David John Browning is a retired obstetrician and gynaecologist. He was educated at Lewes County Grammar School and Guy's Hospital, London. His parents and seven siblings migrated to Australia in 1960. He and his wife followed in 1966. He was in rural general practice for two years before returning to England for specialist training and thence specialist practice in rural NSW.

David John Browning

Tales From
a Women's Doctor

AUSTIN MACAULEY PUBLISHERS™
LONDON • CAMBRIDGE • NEW YORK • SHARJAH

A CIP catalogue record for this title is available from the British Library.

ISBN 9781035800216 (Paperback)
ISBN 9781035800223 (ePub e-book)

www.austinmacauley.com

First Published 2023
Austin Macauley Publishers Ltd®
1 Canada Square
Canary Wharf
London
E14 5AA

I would like to acknowledge the assistance of:

Rev Dick Lucas for taking out the time to write a foreword for my book.

I would like to urge my readers to be so kind and make a donation to our African charity which provides maternal care for the poorest women in a number of East African countries. Further information can be gleaned from https://www.barbaramayfoundation.com

Table of Contents

Foreword

Dr David Browning's vivid account of life and work as a medical specialist (in student terminology Obs and Gynae) is both illuminating and a happy one. And this even for such as myself, and those like me, for whom a description of the ills and operations he daily dealt with is sufficient to cause us to faint outright! What warms the heart of the Christian believer (at the same time making for deep sadness for a secular society) is the evident love of God and grace of our Lord Jesus Christ that lie at the heart of David's achievement, his family and future.

Introduction

The birth of a child is nothing short of miraculous. As an obstetrician I have observed over 10,000 births. The wonder surrounding each new arrival never diminished. Even though I knew much about the mechanisms involved, particularly the change in the circulation of the blood, it never ceased to amaze me that nearly always that change happened without a hitch.

At birth, every baby is presented with a host of new sensations. The most prominent is light. The safe environment of the mother's womb is one of darkness. The new environment outside the womb is full of new challenges. But those challenges are bathed in light. And that light provides the means whereby those challenges can be met. In short, it is the light of life.

There is an even greater force which helps us through life's challenges. That is the spirit of God, the Holy Spirit who guides us to maturity and fills us with purpose and meaning. As they care their patients, doctors will experience sadness and joy, triumphs and failures, heartache and relief. Each new encounter gives impetus to reflection and moulding of character.

It is apposite that both the physical birth of a child and the growth of the personality to its fullest potential should be described as out of darkness into the light of life.

A Beginning

As an obstetrician it was always a great privilege to be present when many little babies made their entry into the world. Often my thoughts would go to their future. What would be this baby boy or baby girl's contribution to society? What career would each one follow? What influences would come to bear on that decision? Of course there are many. But it was always a joy to learn many years later that young so and so had excelled in his or her chosen profession.

Children often follow their parents in the same business, trade or profession. They receive guidance from their schoolteachers and they may undergo various aptitude tests. One strong influence which guides children is their reading material. Favourite characters are quickly identified. Childhood heroes are compelling and romantic. They become a formative part of the years ahead. My heroes were two medical missionaries.

David Livingstone was a Scottish physician and pioneer Christian missionary with the London Missionary Society. He became a legendary explorer in East Africa in the second half of the nineteenth century.

Albert Schweitzer was a theologian, organist, writer, philosopher and, above all, a physician. He founded and sustained a hospital in Lambarene in French Equatorial Africa in the first half of the twentieth century.

As I read the biographies of those two doctors my mind was filled with pictures of them working to heal the sick in that dark and steamy continent. The accounts so enthralled me that, from the age of ten, I was determined to become a doctor too. I never wavered in that desire. There had been no other doctors in the family, although my mother was a nurse.

My secondary education was at Lewes County Grammar School, a state school in the county of Sussex. The A level subjects were the equivalent of the first MB, the studies in the pure sciences required for the Bachelor of Medicine. The time came to decide which university to apply for. The headmaster advised me to take the Cambridge entrance exam, which I did. However my father, being driven by economic considerations, wanted me to enter the workforce as soon as possible. So I went straight to London as the Cambridge course would take one year longer.

Then came the day when I would go for interviews prior to entering medical school. Having been brought up on a dairy farm my father directed that I wear a sports jacket and flat hat, or "Andy Cap", that being the smart attire for a country lad. I arrived first at King's College Hospital in Denmark Hill in south-east London. There, confronted by a phalanx of wise, senior consultants I was quizzed about my reasons for wanting to enter a medical career. I spoke of my two heroes and indicated that I wanted to follow their examples. The consultants very sensibly pointed to my unrealistic and romantic notions. They failed my interview, and I was shown the door.

Later that same day I faced a similar group of wise and senior consultants at Guy's Hospital in Bermondsey, near London Bridge. This time I was better prepared and gave more credible reasons for wanting to be a doctor. And the consultants agreed that I should commence studies at their prestigious hospital and medical school. I later recalled what a privilege it was to be interviewed by such eminent men, as indeed they were.

Guy's Hospital Medical School is part of London University. The course consisted of the second MB which lasted 18 months and then three years of clinical medicine. A lot of study was crammed into those four and a half years and in the last three we were only permitted to take two weeks' holiday per year. The second MB consisted of the basic medical sciences, anatomy, physiology and biochemistry which were digested in those 18 months. We spent many days in the dissecting room where we sat around a cadaver gradually unravelling the complexities of the arteriovenous and nervous systems and the individual muscles. I remember that the ambience of the dissecting room with its rows of cadavers stimulated conversations touching existentialism and related topics. We were privileged to have some very fine demonstrators with us. They filled the roles of tutors. One, who happened to be a fine Christian, later became a professor of surgery and an eminent member of the House of Lords.

Lectures were conducted in classic tiered theatres which were built more than 150 years previously. I imagined the many who had sat there before me on those hard wooden benches. One of the past students was John Keats; but sadly he did not complete his studies. Perhaps he could not keep his mind off his poetry! Our studies in the three subjects were intense and for many weeks prior to the second MB exam we all had our heads in the books for about 13 hours every day.

As soon as we entered the clinical years we were given responsibilities with the patients. Our tasks included keeping some of the medical records and doing the basic pathology tests such as the analysis of the urine and the haemoglobin estimations. Ours was the job of taking blood samples for all other tests to go to the laboratory. There were opportunities to gain a rapport with the patients. Usually they were pleased to pour out their woes to us and they were often more frank with us than with their consultant. Thus we began to understand the physical and emotional suffering which accompanied the various illnesses we encountered.

There were lectures to attend in all branches of medicine and surgery. Pathology lectures could be entertaining. Our mentor in forensic pathology was also the Home Office Pathologist. He was called out to investigate the most gruesome and notorious murders. His lectures were illustrated with slides of those scenes, and he would drily comment about a particularly gory picture, in classic understatement: 'I think there has been some hanky-panky!' Post-mortem examinations were invariably carried out in the lunch hour. They were always instructive, and the forensic ones were particularly interesting. The only snag was that if we were to avoid being reprimanded for lateness at the afternoon lectures we had to eat our sandwiches in the mortuary – or go without lunch. "Bon appétit" could only be said in jest as a post-mortem dissection was invariably associated with unpleasant aromas!

Jennifer Worth's memoirs[1] have been dramatised on television in the "Call the Midwife" series. The action is centred in the suburb of Poplar which is north of the river. The period is the late 50s and early 60s. My experience in Bermondsey, just south of the Thames, was not dissimilar and was also in the early 60s. When a patient failed to appear at the antenatal clinic, a student was dispatched to her home. The hospital owned bicycles for transport. They were painted in the hospital colours and so, if stolen, were easily retrieved. But they had no brakes, no lights and no bells. We carried a bag containing a sphygmomanometer to check the blood pressure and also urine testing sticks. Manoeuvring through London traffic required a little "je ne sais quoi".

The police were very sympathetic. I was returning from a party late one night and had no lights on my own bike. A bobby stopped me and asked where I was from. 'Guy's hospital,' I said very firmly.

'Then you must be after an obstetric case sir. Off you go, sir,' was his kind reply.

One morning I was riding along Tooley Street towards London Bridge. There was a row of parked cars on my side of the road and next to it was a line of stationery traffic. I rode between the two and did not see a pedestrian crossing the road till it was too late. He was carrying a tray of empty teacups from his workplace in a warehouse to my right to a café on my left. I hit him with my bike and, to my horror,

---

[1] Jennifer Worth – "Call the Midwife" – Weidenfeld & Nicholson, London

found he was knocked out cold. Someone from the café came to my aid and together we carried him into the café where we laid him on a bench. Someone else phoned for an ambulance. I went with him in the ambulance to the casualty ward at Guy's hospital. By that stage he had come to. I expected that he would be observed for a few hours at least and was most surprised when the casualty officer swiftly discharged him. At that stage, the police caught up with me and demanded to see my "vehicle". I had a ride in the police car to the "scene of the crime" whereupon the officer tested my brakes. 'These seem to be alright, sir,' he exclaimed – and dismissed me. I was naturally concerned for the victim of the accident and visited him later in his workplace – which happened to be a warehouse loaded with French wine…

A second incident also occurred in Tooley Street. I was walking to my lodgings near Tower Bridge one December evening when I came across a gentleman lying in the gutter. He was moaning and his head was bleeding quite profusely. He had evidently cut his head on the curbing. He needed stitching and I escorted him to the casualty ward. On the way, he repeated four words, over and over again. "Don't tell my wife". Evidently he had imbibed far too much at his office Christmas party in the city. He had staggered over London Bridge on his way to catch his commuter train at London Bridge station. But in his alcoholic stupor he had turned into Tooley Street instead of the station forecourt a few yards further on.

The preparation of a student for medical practice consists of many facets. The generation of stamina was one aspect some senior specialist trainees were very keen to inculcate.

One particular surgical registrar, who was close to receiving his fellowship of the royal college, insisted that we join him for ward rounds after an evening emergency operating list. It was close to midnight. He was bright-eyed and bushy-tailed and expected the same of us. But we were decidedly bleary. The late-night ward round was his way of training us for the long and irregular hours we would soon experience.

There was no delay in starting the real work. As soon as a pass in the final MB BS exam was confirmed we all left the alma mater for the world of hard labour. In the first year after leaving medical school, it was routine to do six months as a house surgeon and six months a house physician. These are junior resident positions. I elected to leave London and work in a provincial town. My choice was Chichester, the cathedral town of Sussex. My duties for the first six months included the follow up of all patients admitted under the care of one general surgeon, two orthopaedic surgeons and one physical medicine specialist (rheumatologist). Also I was on call on alternate nights and alternate weekends in the casualty department.

The workload was therefore heavy and some weeks I was on my feet for more than 100 hours! (What did I do for the other 68 hours some bright spark asked.) This did mean that I benefited by a massive learning curve. The experiences in medical school were largely theoretical. But as a junior resident I took responsibility for decisions which affected the patient's treatment. At first, the senior resident, the registrar, would expect me to ask for his advice quite often. But the expectation was that calling for advice, particularly at dead of night, would become less and less frequent as the weeks went by and I gained more confidence in my decision making.

As time went on I was given more experience. The registrar invited me to take out an acute appendix from a 16-year-old, but, nevertheless, under his close supervision. Unfortunately, it proved to be very unusual, and the consultant had to be called as the appendix was huge and the nearby caecum (large bowel) was also severely swollen. The consultant removed most of the caecum with the appendix. The pathologist diagnosed sarcoidosis which is very rare.

The hospital treated a surprising variety of complex surgical problems. For example, I was an assistant when a thoracic surgeon and an ENT specialist reconstructed a damaged trachea. My job was simply to hold the retractor so that the surgeons could gain better access; but it was a privilege to observe an intricate operation at close quarters and to have a bird's eye view of the anatomy. A young lady had suffered a transection of her trachea from being propelled through the windscreen of her car one year previously. She had been managed with a tracheostomy since the accident. The operation was a lengthy one and all except the anaesthetist – and the patient – broke off for lunch halfway through the procedure.

As a house physician I also experienced a great variety of medical problems. The consultant physicians were excellent teachers, as were the consultant surgeons and registrars. Once I was reprimanded by the medical registrar for not calling her in the wee small hours. She rightly expected me to call her for a life-threatening condition as indeed this was. A lady in her eighties was admitted in a coma. There was no history of any chronic illness. It was soon apparent that she was in diabetic coma. Her blood sugar was sky-high, and she had severe keto-acidosis. With appropriate rehydration, correction of her acidic state and the administration of insulin she was "as right as rain" by breakfast time.

After only 12 months of practice in the hospital, I was able, or perhaps I should say "licenced", to work on my own. A dear friend of the family was a long-established GP (general physician). He had a mixed urban and rural practice on his own in the southeast outskirts of London. He was very keen to trust me with his patients while he went on holiday. I always thought he might have been too trusting; but fortunately there were no bad outcomes. He even asked me to repeat the performance one year later!

My next hospital appointment was as a casualty officer for six months in a southeast London hospital. There I gained experience in setting fractured bones and in a multitude of other injuries. There were even two instances of attempted murder with both the victims and assailants arriving at my casualty department!

The first case involved a jilted lover. In his suburb, as was the case for most of London, there were mainly two storey terraced houses. He had climbed up the drainpipe and entered by a bedroom window. He carried a Smith and Wesson revolver with all six chambers loaded. His former girlfriend was asleep in bed. I imagine she woke with great alarm and sat up as he entered the room. But she had no time to escape from his evil intent. At close range, he squeezed the trigger six times. One bullet took off the tip of her right thumb; the second bullet scored a central hit in her right hand, passing straight through it; another bullet lodged in her right shoulder; the fourth passed through the right side of the abdomen and with the remaining two rounds he missed her body completely.

The assailant then threw himself out of the window and broke a couple of bones on the pavement below. Both he and his victim were West Indians as was a large part of the population in that suburb. Both were transported in the same ambulance. Fortunately, none of the injuries was serious. The abdominal wound was potentially the worst; but when we examined the inside of the lady's abdomen on the operating table we found that all the organs were intact!

The second attempted murder happened in a pub. Again it involved West Indians. One man struck another forcefully in the back with a knife. It was a downward thrust and fortunately the tip of the knife skidded down the shoulder blade and never therefore entered the chest cavity. The victim must have had very good reflexes. He grabbed a heavy piece of wood (perhaps it was a baseball bat), swung backwards with all his might and struck the assailant on the head, knocking him to the floor. Again the two arrived in our casualty ward in one ambulance. Neither of them had serious injuries.

A man in his late fifties was an habitué at the local pub on Saturday nights. His wife strongly suspected he was being unfaithful to her. One particular night he did not return till well after closing time and the wife's suspicions of a dalliance rose to fever pitch. She went into the kitchen and selected the sharpest knife. She lay in wait for his return. When he staggered in full of grog, she deftly relieved him of his pants and with a swift blow struck at his private parts.

Blood gushed over the carpeted floor, and she called for the ambulance. The penis was almost completely severed and there was a large gash in the scrotum. The high blood alcohol level had numbed the pain; but had increased the blood loss. He was duly resuscitated, and the organ was reattached. Healing occurred; but it was doubtful whether there would be any function to satisfy a future dalliance.

The wife was theoretically in mortal danger. Henry VIII had enacted legislation which determined that anyone who rendered a man incapable of fathering a child would suffer the death penalty. Henry was being threatened by France and Spain and wanted sufficient able-bodied men to fill his army. Unfortunately that bill was still on the statute books in 1966. The lady was found guilty of inflicting serious bodily harm; but was spared the death penalty.

I acted in a locum capacity at another SE London hospital for a few weeks. There we received three men who were involved in an accident at a military research establishment not far from the hospital. They were experimenting with a new rocket propellant and all three were exposed to a noxious gas. The cold war was on, and the arms race was in evidence. Two of the three were civilian high-speed photographers. These men were stooped and when invited to sit would not stay still. They had fear written across their faces. They were terrified they were going to die. The third man was a senior naval officer, resplendent in his uniform, standing straight with an air of command. Although he did know some of the military secrets, he was at first totally reluctant to divulge any information.

I needed to know what chemical we were dealing with. Without that information I could offer no treatment other that give oxygen by face mask. The naval officer suggested I spoke to the war office in Whitehall. Getting through to the relevant department took some time. Eventually I received the following advice. 'I am sorry, sir, we have no information about the gas you refer to. You will have to speak to the defence department in the Pentagon in Washington DC.' By that stage, I felt the men would at least show some signs of poisoning. The anxiety expressed by the two photographers persisted; but no other signs appeared.

Then the naval officer volunteered that the gas was a fluorine compound. As a precaution I gave all three a dose of calcium. Calmness supervened at last, and the men were discharged.

My fourth and last junior hospital appointment was at a very busy maternity unit during which I studied and passed the diploma exam in obstetrics. All the foregoing experience enabled me to commence work as a GP in a rural practice. My wife and I migrated to Australia where we joined the rest of my family, my parents and seven younger siblings. They had left the farm in Sussex and migrated six years previously. After a short while in Armidale in northern New South Wales, my father had bought a property, including an apple orchard, just south of Uralla. A doctor on his own in Guyra, just north of Armidale was very keen to find an assistant. There I was given responsibility for the patients in the local cottage hospital as well as in the general practice. I was expected to give anaesthetics, set fractures and take X-rays. House calls could be way out in the bush.

I gained more experience in a group practice in Singleton in the Hunter valley. None of the GPs I met had a diploma in obstetrics and in Singleton I was looked on as an expert in that field. I protested that that was not the case as the diploma only required six months hospital experience in the subject. At that time, there were no actual specialists in rural towns and as I developed further interests in obstetrics and gynaecology I decided to train as a specialist.

That necessitated returning to England for four years before setting up specialist practice in Australia.

The foregoing has described some of my own experiences in equipping me to become a practitioner in my chosen field. First there was the knowledge which was crammed in piece by piece into my grey matter. Then there was the practical experience and associated tuition obtained in hospital appointments. Thirdly there was the gradual development of empathy and understanding which is necessary for a good bedside manner. There were no lectures for this last and most important attribute of a good physician. Doctors acquire these qualities by what some call "osmosis". It means that it is a haphazard and random process. Inevitably some will be heralded as "good doctors" by their patients and others will not be held in such high regard. The yardstick patients will most commonly use is whether their doctor is sympathetic and a good communicator.

There has been only one person who has understood other peoples' needs perfectly and has shown totally consistent and perfect compassion. That person is Jesus Christ. To have Jesus as a tutor transcends all other teaching experiences.

When I first arrived in London as a medical student, my biblical knowledge was minimal, and I had no appreciation of the claims of Jesus Christ. I certainly had no idea that Jesus loved me and what that actually meant. I was blessed with the friendship of several Christian medical and dental students who encouraged me to go to church with them. That meant I was privileged to hear three of the greatest preachers of the mid twentieth century. Rev John Stott was the rector of All Souls, Langham Place, close to the BBC building. Dr Martyn Lloyd-Jones was the minister in charge of Westminster Chapel, near Buckingham Palace. The third was the Rev Dick Lucas who was the rector of St Helen's Bishopsgate. A lot of what they said must have seeped into my brain; but real conviction came through three special encounters.

The first was when a new-found Australian friend met me on the steps of the hospital and explained the truth about the grace of our Lord Jesus Christ. He affirmed the Apostle Paul's statement, 'By grace you have been saved through faith, and this is not your own doing; it is the gift of God.'[2] As we conversed on the steps in semi-darkness the truth of the Gospel burst upon me in glorious light. How could I have been so dull? How could I not have understood the meaning of the amazing grace which those preachers must have stressed?

The two of us marked the fiftieth anniversary of the meeting on the steps of Guy's hospital with a coffee and very encouraging chat in the Royal Botanical Gardens in Sydney.

The second encounter was at a weekend conference of our Christian Union. Our guest speaker, Rev Alan Stibbs, drew the contrast between the Old Testament sacrifices and the sacrifice of Christ. His talks centred on the epistle to the

---

[2] Ephesians 2: 8, New Revised Standard Version

Hebrews. After the Saturday sessions, I was alone in my room and meditating on his beautiful expositions. Quite suddenly I was overcome by an appreciation of the love of Christ. The fact that He should stoop to love me so dearly, as I now was convinced He did, quite overwhelmed me. How did I deserve such love?

The third encounter occurred while I was reading the daily portion prescribed by the "Search the Scriptures" program. The Bible passage was in the Gospel of Luke chapter 4. As an introduction to Jesus' three-year ministry Luke recounts a visit to the synagogue in Nazareth. Jesus is given the scroll of the prophet Isaiah and He finds the place where it is written, 'The Spirit of the Lord is upon me because he has anointed me to bring good news to the poor. He has sent me to proclaim release to the captives and recovery of sight to the blind, and to let the oppressed go free, to proclaim the year of the Lord's favour.[3]' Jesus had applied the prophecy to Himself. In that instant of divine revelation, the freedom Jesus proclaimed meant to me much more than release from guilt and shame. It meant supremely that I was free to be the very person He, Jesus, has created me to be. I no longer needed to model myself on any of my heroes. I could just be myself. Moreover I had a strong conviction of being very precious to Jesus. This filled me with indescribable excitement. I had difficulty in putting it into words (I still do); but I felt an irresistible compulsion to run down the stairs and into the street (Tower Bridge Road) and then relay my staggering revelation to the first passer-by I met. Very fortunately for them, at that precise moment, a

---

[3] Luke 4: 18, 19 New Revised Standard Version

close Christian friend came up to the front door and I was able to tell him about my ecstatic experience.

There then followed experiences which confirmed that Jesus through His Spirit was indeed tutoring me.

A Christian friend invited me to join a Children's Special Service Mission event in Montrose on Scotland's east coast during the summer holiday. We ministered to a group of rowdy Glasgow primary age children. The activities were mostly on the beach. But Scotland's notorious inclement summer weather meant some activities had to be arranged indoors. We had the use of school buildings. There the leader asked me to speak to a large number of the children and give them a word picture of the first Good Friday. I got them to imagine, as they sat on the floor in front of me, that they observed the scene from a high vantage point such as the pinnacle of the temple. I have to say that I had never spoken in public before. In my own school days, one particular failing was the inability to be coherent in a class discussion.

The leader had unbelievable faith in me. Even though it is over 60 years ago, I can still remember clearly two things about that assignment. As I stood in front of all those children I spotted the leader through the open door to the classroom. He was obviously praying. And then as I spoke there was complete silence. The children's eyes were fixed on me. They were totally absorbed in what I was saying. I had no visual aids. I could not believe it. It had to be the work of the Holy Spirit. What a tutor! What a mentor! What a transformation!

Later I was asked by the chaplain at Guy's hospital to assist with church services on the wards. It was the custom to conduct services on Saturday or Sunday evenings. If possible, every patient in the hospital should be able to witness a church service every weekend. Each service lasted 15 minutes and was then repeated in three other wards. The routine was hymn, Bible reading, address and prayer. The fierce ward sisters were adamant that we do not exceed 15 minutes in all. The patients mostly looked forward to the service; but there was little time to speak to them individually. There would be other opportunities to speak with them and I am sure many were comforted by our brief services. Later conversations revealed that many patients did indeed appreciate our ministry.

Both of these experiences were invaluable in teaching me ways to approach the spiritual component of my patients' lives. Each five-minute address needed much prayerful preparation. I firmly believe that without the guidance and tuition of the Holy Spirit I would not be able to appreciate the inner fears and anxieties of my patients as I should. I would not be able to truly empathise as I should. And even then I would fall way short of the example my Lord and Master has given me.

My Christian faith proved to be a bulwark to help me through the trials and tribulations that would face me in the ensuing years.

Sadness and Joy

Most women approach their first labour with a degree of trepidation. Even the word "labour" dispels any thought of pleasure. Many remember God's injunction 'In pain you shall bring forth children.'[4] Uterine contractions are very definitely painful, and the tearing of soft tissues can be excruciating.

Soon after I commenced work as GP in Guyra I witnessed an unusually straightforward birth. The mother conducted herself with barely a whimper. Minimal pain relief was requested, and minimal relief was administered. The actual birth was so well controlled that I encouraged the mother to place her hands on the baby's head and gently complete the delivery herself. All in attendance were amazed and overjoyed. The happy event was immediately announced in the local paper, the proud father being the paper's editor.

That happy event gave me encouragement to think that all confinements in this lucky country would be easy and painless. That of course was not the case. Every subsequent mother experienced a variable degree of pain. But almost all

---

[4] Genesis 3: 16

forgot the pain and expressed great joy when they held their new-born child in their arms. Jesus reminded us of the normal course of events when he said, 'When a woman is in labour she has pain because her hour has come. But when her child is born she no longer remembers the anguish because of the joy of having brought a human being into the world.'[5]

Unless she is living in total isolation every young mother has heard horror stories. Although the vast majority of pregnancies and births are straightforward, there is a small number of babies who die before and after birth. And there are a small number of pregnancies which are attended by serious complications. The death of the mother is much less common; but we must always be on the lookout for complications and take appropriate action.

The role of the obstetrician is to attend to complications. Normal births can and should be left to midwives. That means that the obstetrician will experience a much higher proportion of the "sad" cases.

Because complications can occur without warning, mothers in Western countries have been advised to give birth in hospital. For many years, homebirths in Australia have amounted to about 0.3% of the total number of deliveries. In the USA, the figure for 2015 was 2.3%. In recent years, similar figures were recorded in the UK. But in 1960 33.2% of births occurred at home in the UK. Then a rapid reduction in home births was promoted and in 1970 the figure dropped to 12.7%.

---

[5] John 16:21

In the 1960s and 70s in England, every maternity hospital organised a "Flying Squad". This was designed to respond to an emergency when a complication occurred at home. Most commonly it was a haemorrhage. My first experience was a case of heavy bleeding with a miscarriage. I was the house surgeon (junior doctor) and went out from the hospital by ambulance. On that occasion, it was an unpleasant experience because the old Bedford ambulances had very soft springs. Travelling in the back of the vehicle swiftly brought on motion sickness. Weaving through the back streets of SE London as quickly as the driver could manage made the affliction a certainty.

The patient with the haemorrhage looked very pale. I, as the young junior doctor, arrived with a matching skin colour! But in spite of my discomfort I had to go to work and resuscitate the patient. The bleeding had almost stopped after the administration of ergometrine and with an intravenous infusion in place the patient was out of danger. The ambulance driver chose a much more comfortable speed for the return journey.

Another nauseating trip was for a supposed large post-partum haemorrhage. A baby had been safely delivered by the district midwife with the GP in attendance. There was no sign of the placenta (afterbirth) arriving. The GP noted the mother's uterus (womb) to be unusually large at this stage and assumed it was full of blood. He administered ergometrine to reduce bleeding and called for the "Flying Squad".

On our arrival, we found the mother to be in fine fettle. She had a good colour and normal pulse rate and blood pressure. There were none of the expected signs of

31

haemorrhage. Examination of the uterus revealed it to be still as large as an undelivered pregnancy. It did not require much lateral thinking to conclude that we had an undiagnosed twin. So the next thing to do was to listen for the baby's heartbeat. Unfortunately, that could not be found. I had to explain the situation as diplomatically as possible. We had a mother with an unborn dead baby, killed by the administration of ergometrine. And the GP was understandably distressed by his mistaken diagnosis.

The pace was leisurely for the return journey. On arrival at the hospital delivering the dead baby with the cervix (neck of the womb) clamped down under the influence of the ergometrine proved very difficult. A general anaesthetic was employed. The mother recovered quickly and could soon return home with her healthy live baby.

At another hospital, the registrar, a more senior doctor, was assigned to take responsibility for flying squad calls. Also we were to use our own cars. That meant we needed "The Knowledge". Like London taxi drivers we had to have the local map printed on our grey matter. We had to find our way to the emergency as quickly as possible. (There was no GPS in those days).

One case was a large post-partum haemorrhage. An experienced midwife had delivered a healthy baby. The placenta came away normally. The uterus was contracted down; but heavy bleeding followed. This was the mother's third or fourth baby and she had no problems with the previous births.

The hospital midwife and I climbed the narrow stairs up to the bedroom and found the mother in poor shape. The domiciliary midwife, with the help of the husband, had elevated the foot of the bed, but the blood pressure was still very low. In fact, horror of horrors, it was not possible to get a reading at all. It was imperative to restore the hugely diminished blood volume as soon as possible. To that end we infused two litres of saline, two bottles of a plasma substitute and two pints of uncross-matched O-negative blood. But still the blood pressure was unrecordable. What could we do? We had used all the intravenous fluids we carried and still the patient was in bad shape. The bleeding had stopped and with that information we received consultant advice to transport the patient to hospital.

We carried her headfirst down the narrow stairs. At this point, she was almost vertical. By the time she reached the ground floor, she had improved. The pulse was stronger. We gained more confidence in the resuscitation and bundled her into a waiting ambulance.

Under an anaesthetic the source of the bleeding was identified. There had been a large laceration (tear) of the cervix. This had very likely been caused during delivery of the baby's shoulders. The laceration was repaired with heavy soluble sutures, and all was well. We were able to heave a sigh of relief and marvel at the resilience of this young mother.

Another case added some gentle humour to our busy lives. There had been a normal birth of a healthy baby. But the placenta was reluctant to leave its mooring of the previous nine months in spite of nature's prompting and the midwife's urging. So she called the flying squad.

It was the policy at that hospital to remove a retained placenta in the patient's home. The reason is that uterine bleeding is more likely to occur when the patient is moved with the placenta still in place.

Three people were required to respond to the flying squad call in this instance, the obstetric registrar (myself), a hospital midwife and an anaesthetist. A simple, portable anaesthetic machine was used. The midwife carried the kit required by the obstetrician. The team of three plus all the "gear" was crammed into a bedroom high up in a block of flats. The room was sparsely furnished because the double bed occupied most of the available space.

The district midwife noted that a flat in a neighbouring block was owned by a certain Ronnie Corbett. As the anaesthetist tried to put the patient to sleep we all began to giggle! No one, but no one, had checked the anaesthetic machine before we left the hospital. No one had noticed that there was a hole in the rubber tubing. The small bedroom quickly filled with nitrous oxide, laughing gas. The only person not laughing was the patient. She was still wide awake and not a little apprehensive. We reassured her.

The anaesthetist was quick to cut off the perished area of tubing, reattach the shortened tube and start the anaesthetic again. The patient went dutifully to sleep, and the placenta was removed.

I was once called to a similar, though more serious complication, about 400 kms from the nearest hospital. Six of us were visiting the Presbyterian mission station, Ernabella, in the Musgrave ranges in NW South Australia. My youngest brother was teaching the local Pitjantjatjara cattle work. At about 3.00 a.m., I was woken by a midwife who had just delivered an aboriginal of a healthy baby. But the afterbirth was stuck, and she started to bleed heavily. We were at the out station, Fregon, where there were little resources to assist in any serious complication. We certainly could not give an anaesthetic. A blood transfusion could only be given in Alice Springs. However, at the main station, Ernabella, there was a stock of serum albumen, a blood substitute. My brother raced the 70 kms to fetch it and that helped to restore the blood volume. With a lot of coaxing, the placenta was eventually delivered; but we could not be sure if it was complete.

About halfway through the morning my father, who was traveling with us, came up to me and asked boldly, 'Is she dead yet?'

'No, Dad,' I said very confidently. 'She is not going to die.' She did however rapidly become very anaemic and probably lost about half her blood volume. At about 3.00 p.m., I assessed that she was well enough to be transported. We carried her on a stretcher in the back of the Ute with my brother driving. 70 kms up the track we met the flying doctor who flew her to Alice Springs. There she was given a blood transfusion and curettage to remove remnants of the placenta. A happy mother was eventually returned to Ernabella.

The Pitjantjatjara people remembered that complication for many years. 20 years after the event my wife and I were attending the Flynn Memorial Church in Alice Springs. An Aboriginal lady spoke to us afterwards and reminded me of the help I had given.

Although rare, all manner of incidental complications can occur in a pregnancy. One such complication is the dreaded big "C".

35

Cervical cancer is caused by an infection with the wart virus and is now being very effectively screened by detecting the presence of the virus. Moreover the incidence of cervical cancer is falling rapidly with the introduction of the vaccine against human papilloma virus infection. Previously the PAP smear was the first line of detection. Before the development of colposcopy, a positive PAP smear was followed up with a cone biopsy. As its name suggests a cone shaped piece was cut from the uterine cervix and examined under the microscope. If there was no invasive cancer that biopsy was curative.

A lady with a positive PAP smear presented at a well-known city women's hospital. She was two months pregnant and was advised to undergo a cone biopsy. She was found to have a pre-malignant condition and did not require any further treatment. Unfortunately, she miscarried a few days later. In her second pregnancy, the waters broke at five months. She was rested but the pregnancy became infected, and the baby died. There was a stillbirth at $6^1/_2$ months.

It became obvious that the large cone biopsy had severely weakened the cervix (neck of the womb) and it would be very unlikely that she would ever carry a baby right through a pregnancy. The usual practice in such cases is to stitch the cervix at about three months of the pregnancy. But because such a large piece of the cervix had been removed I decided to insert a supporting suture before conception. Also the lady was fast approaching 40 years of age.

The suture was successful, and she carried the next pregnancy to $8^1/_2$ months when the waters broke. The baby was in the breech position, and we opted for a Caesarean section. (The stitch was still in the neck of the womb). The timing for this emergency was not good for the doctors and other staff. It was late on Christmas Eve. However the timing added eternal significance for the new parents.

One more medical challenge presented itself. The patient proved to be very difficult to anaesthetise and there was rising concern for the welfare of the baby because of the delay. When a second anaesthetist was sent for, there was a definite crescendo in my anxiety level. However I was able to deliver the baby safely. There was no evidence of oxygen deprivation. Anxiety changed to joy and thankfulness. The parents enjoyed the best possible Christmas present with their new-born boy.

One particularly sad case began when a mother noted a painful swelling on her right knee. She was about to experience a complication as rare as the proverbial hen's teeth. She was five months pregnant. Investigation revealed the worst possible diagnosis, a synovial sarcoma. This is a malignant tumour of the lining of the joint. It was life threatening. Drastic measures were called for. The leg was amputated at mid-thigh. This left her with a good prognosis. But she had an uphill battle to adjust to mobility with one leg and an advancing pregnancy. She expected to receive appropriate support, particularly from her husband. But he no longer liked what he saw. He shut his eyes to her beautiful personality and her obvious fortitude. He could not face the responsibility of caring for a wife with this extra burden. So he opted to leave and find another woman who would satisfy his (selfish) needs.

The dear lady soldiered on. Fortunately, the pregnancy was otherwise uncomplicated. But the birth was particularly difficult with only one leg. I remember very clearly her attempts to bear down and my having to support her right side as she progressed in the second stage of labour. She managed it well and a healthy-looking baby was born without any surgical assistance. Mother and child bonded well, and the new baby compensated to a degree for her recent losses.

Disaster struck again three months after the birth. The baby succumbed to a "cot death". No one was to blame, least of all the mother. At that time, there were only theories: Research had as yet not found a definitive cause.

My abiding memory is of a beautiful personality and my prayer was that she would find a genuine supporting companion in place of her errant husband.

I was left with a philosophical question. Why was one person subjected to so many disasters? This lady lost a leg, a husband and a baby in quick succession. It sounds more than anyone could possibly bear. As physicians we are called on not only to treat the physical disease but also to encourage the person to find the necessary strength. Healing is effected not just with medicines and bandages but also with emotional and spiritual support. I felt emotionally drained and was therefore impotent to provide her help. It was she who proved, by God's providence, to have gained that inner strength.

Another very sad case was when a baby failed to breath after a difficult delivery. When the baby's head is deep in the pelvis and there is delayed progress in the birth, we expect that the delivery can be completed with the help of obstetric forceps or the vacuum extractor. In this case, I needed to apply more traction on the forceps than I expected.

The baby's colour at birth was quite good but he made no attempt to breath. I ventilated the baby and the lungs expanded normally; but still there was no sign of spontaneous respiration. I phoned the Children's Hospital in Camperdown, Sydney. I felt I had no choice but to personally accompany the baby on the 120 kms road journey to the Children's Hospital while ventilating artificially all the time. Unfortunately, there was nothing they could do, and the baby succumbed. There had been a transection of the spinal cord which is a very rare complication. The return journey and conversation with the mother and father were particularly difficult. All the empathy I could muster was necessary in those emotional moments. The parents were amazingly understanding, and I felt I did not deserve such graciousness from them.

Infertility is a source of angst for a large number of women. It was always particularly distressing in ancient cultures and today it is distressing for Africans. In those cultures, a woman's lifetime fulfilment rests entirely on her ability to nurture children. Throughout Western Society the fertility rate is low. The average number of children per female is a little less than two. Nevertheless the urge for motherhood is strong and much effort and expense is given over to treating infertility.

Advances in in-vitro fertilisation (IVF) have ensured that the successful pregnancy rate for the younger infertile couple is very high. But over the maternal age of 35 the success rate diminishes and over 40 there is a steep reduction in that rate. There are many who pursue a career and delay motherhood. In a society that expects instant gratification, it is difficult to keep hope alive. Yet that is one of the duties of the treating physician.

Although the larger numbers of pregnancies in infertile couples are achieved by IVF, methods appropriate to the particular cause of infertility are also used.

One particular lady had been seeing a specialist in the city for some years. She had been through the usual batch of investigations but no cause for her lack of success was identified. Then she developed severe menorrhagia, heavy periods, and it was clear that it was caused by large uterine fibroids which are benign tumours. The uterus (womb) was enlarged to the size of a four-month pregnancy. I organised a myomectomy, the surgical removal of the fibroids. The operation was tedious. To secure good control of bleeding within the uterus I found that a large number of sutures was needed. There were plenty of bleeding points that had to be secured. This made the anaesthetist somewhat impatient! She even made sarcastic remarks about the number of sutures going in! The patient healed quickly. Then, miracle of miracles, she conceived in the very next menstrual cycle! Her excitement was extreme. She and her husband had much to be thankful for. The joy of motherhood had become a reality.

She had three children, all delivered by Caesarean section because of the scar on her uterus and because more fibroids had grown which would have impeded a normal birth.

It must be noted that fibroids pose a rare cause for infertility. They only prevent conception if they distort both the Fallopian tubes (oviducts) to the point of complete blockage.

I am tempted to agree with Oswald Chambers who proclaimed that "Life is more tragic than orderly".[6] It was my job to care for those few mothers who had unhappy outcomes. As much as possible I left the normal pregnancies and straightforward births to the midwives. And so my experience was tilted towards sadness.

Congenital abnormalities in toto are not rare. They are certainly a cause of great sadness. There are a huge number of different inherited diseases, some being relatively common and others being exceedingly rare. There are diseases caused by faulty cell divisions, or mutations, in the current pregnancy. The most common of these is Down's syndrome where the presence of an extra chromosome results in in a variable mental handicap and distinctive facial features.

About one in every thousand pregnancies results in an anencephalic baby. In this instance, there a gross abnormality with most of the brain not being formed at all. The diagnosis is very obvious when an ultrasound examination is performed early in the pregnancy. The baby dies very soon after birth.

Whenever there is a complication or when there is an abnormality or the death of a baby it falls on the obstetrician to give a compassionate explanation to the parents and to be a prime source of comfort. To understand exactly what has happened is a vital step in dealing with grief. One of my tasks was to give a measure of hope for the future. I was always in awe of the childbearing ladies who endured great physical and emotional pain. It is also a privilege to be able

---

[6] My Utmost for His Highest – Oswald Chambers

to observe their relief when pain and sadness is later replaced by hope joy.

The words of Jesus come to mind again. 'When a woman is in labour, she is in pain because her hour has come. But when her child is born she no longer remembers the anguish because of the joy of having brought a human being into the world.'[2] Jesus was signifying His own cruel death and subsequent resurrection. There would be weeping and mourning, great pain and anguish; but the dawn would break replacing it all with rejoicing which would last for ever.

Friday

As the celebration of Easter approached in 1978 it was an enormous privilege for me to be asked to read all the Bible passages for the Good Friday service. This was at the Anglican Church in Bowral. The Rector felt that using just one reader would facilitate everyone's meditation on the events of the first Good Friday. During the service we were all invited to prayerfully reflect on the redemptive work of Christ on the cross and to appropriate His forgiveness for our rebellion. The Rector's sermons on both Good Friday and Easter Day were inspiring. They were, from a spiritual perspective, a preparation for the following Friday. That was the day of the accident.

Three things of note happened on that day. First it was our eldest son's eleventh birthday. Second I sent the largest cheque ever to the tax man. The department was at its most voracious when gathering provisional tax. I was later told that a refund was out of the question and that I would have to wait till the following year to square things with the tax department. Not a grain of sympathy was expressed. The third item was an evening meeting of the local camp of Gideons International which I was assigned to chair. (Gideons is the organisation which places Bibles in hotel and

43

hospital bedside lockers and distributes testaments to students and members of the police and armed forces). My wife was also a member, but she had stayed at home with our three children and the birthday party.

On our return home from the dinner meeting, I was driving with two fellow Gideons. Percy was in the front and Pat, his wife, was seated behind. As we drove gently through the built-up area with the obligatory speed limit we were completely oblivious to the danger ahead.

At the same time, two young men stepped into a fast car. They had been drinking heavily in a local pub. They drove in our direction at speeds, according to one estimate, of up to 160 kms per hour. A friend driving behind us recalls seeing the lights of a car approaching on the wrong side of the road at tremendous speed. They had overtaken another vehicle and hit us head on. All that kinetic energy was transferred to our car as a massive crushing force. Percy, now an elderly man, died at the scene as did the young man in the passenger seat of the oncoming car. The driver of that car and Pat, sitting in the back seat of our car, both escaped with minor injuries. I was trapped by the crushing impact. My driver's side door was folded in half as if it was cardboard, such was the magnitude of the force. The resulting jagged edge projected into my side. My upper thigh took the full impact and the upper third of the femur was shattered into many pieces. With the compression of the car body, the seat belt afforded no protection. Multiple fractures of both upper and lower jaws resulted from sharp contact with the steering wheel. There were many other injuries, some of which were not identified till weeks or years later.

It took the rescue team a long time to cut through the car's mangled bodywork and release me. Although I responded as if conscious, mercifully all memory of the accident was wiped out. So I have no recollection of screaming in pain when I was moved. The ambulance took me to the local hospital where a large team of local doctors including the surgical specialist was poised to assist. Meanwhile a friend went to knock on our front door. My wife had the shock of her life and experienced an even greater shock when she saw me in the hospital.

The first visit to the operating theatre resulted in the repair of multiple lacerations. The next morning I was transferred to the intensive care ward at Royal Prince Alfred Hospital. I was rushed down to Sydney by road ambulance with my wife travelling in the front. I had evidently lost a lot of blood, mainly from the fractured femur. The following day and about 48 hours after the accident my first memory was of one of the doctors taking blood from my radial artery to check the blood gases, the oxygen level etc. I was treated in the intensive care ward and the previous night it was thought I might not survive. During the next few days, my wife travelled in from my aunt's flat in Maroubra Bay where she was lodging. Each journey was, she said, a fearful experience as she wondered what state I would be in when she arrived. As she watched over my broken body she had a very stressful time. She had observed my near fatal injuries and had contemplated life without me. How could she manage with three young children and no income? How could she cope if the very close marriage bond was suddenly severed? Those thoughts were too hard to handle. Our three young children were also very distressed and she had to comfort them as best she could.

She sought comfort and guidance in her Bible and was miraculously led to read James 5:15 'The prayer of faith will save the sick, and the Lord will raise them up.' That gave her the reassurance she desperately needed.

Mercifully, my progress was rapid after the first few days. This gave confidence to my brother, George, when he made an outstanding statement. 'It seems the Lord has something more for you to do!' I felt enormously blessed on hearing those words. It gave me immediate hope for resuming my calling as a specialist obstetrician and gynaecologist.

We were most fortunate that there was a highly skilled maxillo-facial surgeon visiting the hospital from the USA. He mended my broken jaws by inserting many wires. For the next six weeks, I could only have fluids; so purees were the go. I lost a significant amount of weight. There was also the ever-present risk of inhaling vomit. Pliers were always on hand to cut the wires if that occurred.

Under the same anaesthetic as my jaws were mended an orthopaedic surgeon did a preliminary repair of my fractured right femur. I say preliminary, because as he explained, there was so much tissue damage and collection of blood that all he could do was bridge the gap with some metalwork, a Smith Peterson nail. He said the bone would not heal until all the initial traumas had settled. The nail was taking the strain and would eventually fail.

Ironically, metal fatigue revealed itself while I was operating on someone else over eight months later. In the midst of a laparotomy, there was a sudden pang in my upper thigh. I informed the anaesthetist who was most dismissive. 'Don't be ridiculous,' she said. I could not leave the patient's abdomen open and the operation unfinished. The teeth were gritted. The job was completed. Afterwards an x-ray confirmed the broken nail, and I was able to indulge in a smidgen of pride when reporting back to the anaesthetist.

'I told you so.' Putting any weight on the leg was painful and I had to manage with crutches again till another operation could be arranged.

Operation number four involved a bone graft from the top of the hip to the femur. A new Smith Peterson nail was inserted while the bone healed. Operation number five was the removal of the second nail twelve months later. At least, one broken screw from the first operation remained in the bone.

Most of my friends and many patients had gotten used to seeing me with crutches. In fact, I went back to work about six weeks after the accident with crutches and speaking like a Queenslander! (We Mexicans maintain they speak with clenched teeth to keep the flies out). My jaws were wired together tightly to assist healing of the bones. Apparently I was able to make myself understood. But I was not permitted to work in the operating theatre initially because they did not have a big enough autoclave to sterilise my crutches! My third operation was to have the wires removed which made up the scaffolding for the upper and lower jaws. Thereafter there were years of dental work to look forward to!

It is notoriously difficult to measure pain and one has to rely on subjective impressions. Lessons were learnt which would help in understanding the pain experienced by other sufferers. Pain relief was variable. For example, after the bone graft operation I was offered the use of a newly acquired TENS machine over the wound on my thigh. The therapist was upset when I told her that the wound area was numb and that the donor area for the bone graft, the iliac crest, was really painful. 'No we are not allowed to use the TENS on the abdomen,' was the curt reply. The iliac crest is at the edge of the abdomen, and I was not given any effective pain relief for that very sore spot.

CAT scans were not available in 1978 and that is why many of the injuries were not documented at the time. The area which was the seat of more pain than anywhere else was the lumbar part of the spine. I remember that being particularly severe. It seemed the medical attendants expected me to have pain in that area. It was par for the course. Also many years later pain radiated from the neck. It is quite possible that minor fractures occurred in both parts of the spine as well as significant soft tissue injury.

Head injury always causes much concern. Although I did not have objective loss of consciousness, the total loss of memory for 24 hours before and 48 hours after the accident would indicate a serious concussion. Scans, as previously mentioned, were not available and the extent of any possible head injury could not therefore be accurately assessed. Apart from the initial complete memory loss there was one other frightening feature. When I was preparing to go back to work, I discovered to my horror that I had forgotten much of my medical knowledge. How could I continue to treat my patients? At first I wrestled with that thought thinking I might have to resign my position as a specialist obstetrician and gynaecologist and maybe not work as a doctor at all. I remember my mother visiting at Royal Prince Alfred Hospital and being so glad when I showed her that my hands suffered minimal injuries. But what use are clever hands without a resourceful brain? Also I began to question my brother's earlier remark, 'The Lord has something more for you to do.' Would I really be able to be useful to society in the future? Mercifully, the medical knowledge gradually returned to what I assumed was normal for me. Incidentally, some scarring in the left frontal lobe of the brain was discovered many years later.

Blessings abounded during the time of my recovery. All the local churches with their many parishioners upheld me and my family in prayer. The Rector of our own church was very attentive, particularly at the time of the accident when he was a very welcome and strong support for my wife. About six months later he was mowing the grass around the rectory when he suddenly collapsed and died. As we lived quite close to the rectory I was able to be one of the first on the scene to give support to his wife. His death was a massive tragedy for the whole church and the local community.

There were other incidences of acute sadness. Two of my would-be patients, who later became long term friends, suffered stillbirths.

It was important to find a specialist locum as I was the only obstetrician and gynaecologist in town. Very fortunately an English specialist was exploring the Antipodes. He had been on a working holiday, had just completed a stint in New Zealand and was only too pleased to work for us. The patients were assured he was like me; but his wife was a little different. She was a black West

Indian and a concert pianist! There was initially no money to pay the locum and a dear friend lent us sufficient funds to take us past the emergency period.

There was time to reflect. The State of Victoria had introduced random breath testing and it was time that same measure should be introduced into NSW. The death toll on the roads was far too high. I therefore felt compelled to lobby the NSW government. There was an immediate backlash. It was said that it would be an invasion of civil liberties. Angry letters appeared in the press. But fortunately common sense prevailed, and random testing became law. The effect was dramatic. The death toll plummeted.

The driver of the other car stood trial at the district court in Campbelltown. I was called as a witness. As I had no recollection of the accident whatsoever I thought I must be exhibit "A"! All I can remember of the questioning whilst at the witness stand was the defence counsel asking, 'Now doctor, what do you think of the blood sample taken from my client: was the test reliable?' Doubtless blood would have been taken from the driver some considerable time after the accident. An alcohol level of 0.25% was recorded. My understanding is that for the average person 0.35% renders one unconscious and 0.45% is fatal. The district court judge found him guilty of culpable driving and he was sentenced to 18 months in gaol.

Some weeks before the court hearing a most extraordinary thing happened. The father of the other driver contacted us to ask if he could bring his son to see me. It was at the stage when I was at home and before returning to work. There was plenty of evidence of my trauma. Besides the crutches and wires holding the jaws together there was still bruising of my face and elsewhere.

When they arrived, they lost no time in small talk. They had travelled from the far side of Bathurst and made it clear that their mission was to seek my forgiveness. This was the first time I had met the father or the son. It was a most unusual situation. The closest most victims ever get to the one who caused the accident is across the wide expanse of the court room. They do not normally want any closer contact. The priority for most aggrieved people is to secure justice. They want closure and that means they want to know that suitable punishment is carried out. Usually they are not satisfied unless it is the punishment which they themselves prescribe.

As the two men walked into our lounge room my focus was at once on the younger one, the son of only 19 years who had driven that car so recklessly on that fatal night. He had the appearance of youthful innocence. There was no disputing his guilt; but there was also no denying his contrition. He was obviously repentant. Yes, he would face whatever the court decided should be his punishment. But more than anything he wanted to put this episode behind him. Thereafter he sought to restore his life. His first step to restoration was forgiveness from the people he had harmed.

Forgiveness does not deny the guilt; but it does prepare a path to reconciliation. It says in effect, 'I do not condone what you have done, but from now on I do not condemn you. I will not remain angry with you because your need is to be restored. There is no longer any antipathy between us. I extend to you the love Jesus has given me.'

As I looked into his face I wondered how such a pleasant looking young man could have abandoned all good sense. And as my mind went back to that fateful Friday I recalled that it was exactly a week following Good Friday. Because God had then forgiven my rebellion and sinfulness against Him and had given me a new and wonderful life who was I to withhold my forgiveness? I had to forgive that young man. And I did.

Justice is the prerogative of the State – and for the Christian it is the prerogative of the State and God. He must leave it to God and the state-appointed justice system. His responsibility is to offer forgiveness. It is the message of the first Good Friday. On that day Jesus said, from the cross, 'Father, forgive them; for they do not know what they are doing.'[7] Jesus' amazing grace extends life-changing forgiveness to all who seek it. Archbishop Desmond Tutu chaired the Truth and Reconciliation Commission following the collapse of apartheid in South Africa. His conclusion and firm conviction is, 'There is no future without forgiveness.'[8]

C.S. Lewis put it like this: 'To be a Christian means to forgive the inexcusable because God has forgiven the inexcusable.'[9] That is very hard to put into practice.

---

[7] Luke 23: 34

[8] Desmond Tutu – "No Future without Forgiveness" – Random House 1999.

[9] C.S. Lewis – "On Forgiveness" in "The Weight of Glory and Other Addresses" – Collier Books/Macmillan 1980

Helping the Police with
Their Enquiries

'Pull over, Sir,' said the kind policeman. Many others in a stream of traffic had also not observed the speed limit of that short, straight section on the Hume Highway as it passed through the aptly named hamlet of Bookham. The policeman took the details from my driver's licence and consulted his records. He returned with a smile, 'Hello, Dr Browning, how are you? Off you go, sir!' We were 200 kms from home and his wife had evidently been a patient of mine.

All through my professional career I enjoyed a very good relationship with the police, and a few became close friends.

As a surgeon and physician one will become involved with the affairs of the local community, and one will inevitably be called on to give opinions about incidents which have a bearing on the health of individuals. These may be in relation to accidents or even crimes.

As a young GP I was summoned to the local court. Two little boys had been sent into care because their mother had a serious drug problem and was deemed unfit to look after them. The time came for the mother to be reassessed and I was asked to give an appraisal in court. I had examined the mother both from a physical and mental point of view. My conclusion was that she was now capable of caring for her boys once again. I remember the magistrate thanking me for my thorough account.

A sudden and unexpected event can be a shock to a whole community. One such shocking event was when a dog dug up the body of a new-born baby.

At first, there were no clues. It was a mystery. The police conducted a detailed door-knock exercise; but no one had any idea as to the origin of that little body.

Then I was referred a sixteen-year-old girl with what was assumed to be some heavy and prolonged menstrual bleeding. The GP had ordered an ultrasound scan. That showed an enlarged uterus (womb). The report suggested the presence of a fibroid (benign swelling of the muscle). The young lady denied the possibility of pregnancy. Only three weeks previously she had been modelling clothes in a local shopping mall. She appeared with a suitably slim outline.

She needed to have a diagnostic curettage to arrive at a diagnosis and it was then that it became obvious that she had recently given birth. Eventually she confessed to the pregnancy. She confessed too to burying a dead baby. She was very frightened and did not want to share the information with anyone else. No one had guessed she was pregnant, not even her mother. Although the baby was a normal size, she had successfully concealed the pregnancy right up to full term. She had given birth secretly at home.

It was important to guard her privacy, particularly from the press. The police, however, had to conclude their business. Most importantly it had to be established that the baby was dead at birth. It is a crime to conceal a birth, but no crime is committed if it was a stillbirth. I was introduced to a very sensitive and caring lady detective. Together she and I interviewed the young patient. But so as not to give any clues to other patients or even to the hospital staff I escorted her to a private room at the back of the hospital where we met the detective.

The girl's mother was very understanding, and the girl recovered from her ordeal. Some years later I heard she had moved away from the district, was happily married and was starting a family.

In our district, there was more than one institution for children who presented with serious problems with their education. One such was a school for truants. This was a boarding facility and children came from all over the state. A 13-year-old girl was referred to me well into a pregnancy. She was a big girl for her age and had matured early. Her charges at the school concluded that a termination of the pregnancy was the only option. I was not so sure that was correct. The operation might not be straight forward as she was over three months pregnant. There could be lasting complications such as weakening of the neck of the womb and subsequent late miscarriages. I felt other options should at least be discussed.

She was referred to a teaching hospital in Sydney where preparations were made for a termination of the pregnancy. That would be a mid-trimester abortion.

Because she was a minor, consent for the operation had to be obtained from her legal guardian. She was a ward of the state, and her legal guardian was the NSW minister for Family and Community Services. As he was a Roman Catholic he refused to give consent. His opinion was to be challenged in court. Because I was the first doctor to see the young lady and confirm her pregnancy I was asked to give evidence. Prior to my appearance I was sent a document to ascertain my bona fides. That included, amongst other things, an enquiry about my solvency. The document included some archaic expressions. One was an order to list "old socks under the bed". Apparently that meant loose cash!

The court in Sydney did not have the statutory time before the hearing to issue me with a subpoena. Therefore I was not obliged to attend. When I informed them that my medical duties precluded my travelling to Sydney, they said they were prepared to adjourn the hearing to Bowral. At this stage, there was a distinct risk that the case would become an embarrassment to the NSW government. I suspect that the Premier, Neville Wran, intervened. That was because the court hearing was cancelled. In what seemed to me to be a legal irregularity, permission was granted for the termination of the pregnancy to go ahead without any further delay. The operation was safely carried out at the teaching hospital.

One tragedy which can befall an unsuspecting mother is a cot death. The cause of this event had eluded medical science for many years and there was no diminution in its incidence. Greater understanding has taken place more recently.

One young couple had a heroin addiction. They both switched to methadone under medical supervision and that was continued during their first pregnancy. The baby was bottle fed and was under the care of a specialist paediatrician. Careful treatment is necessary to prevent distressing withdrawal symptoms as the level of drugs received from the mother's circulation suddenly falls when the baby is born.

The couple took their baby home, and all was well at first. Follow up visits did not reveal any problems. Then there was an urgent phone call from the mother. She had found the baby dead in bed. It was three months after the birth and the immediate thought was that this was an "ordinary" cot death. However the post-mortem examination revealed a large amount of methadone in the baby's stomach. There was more than enough to explain the death.

Both parents were charged with killing their baby. At the hearing, each one blamed the other for administering a lethal dose of methadone. Unfortunately both parents were represented by the same lawyer; so the magistrate had no option but to dismiss the case.

Actual rape occurs far too often. Each accident and emergency department has a roster of female doctors who can consult and examine rape victims who present of their own volition or who are referred by the police.

I was called as an expert witness in a case of possible rape. The hearing was held in the magnificent court building in Goulburn with judge and jury. The barrister asked me to comment on the testimony of the doctor who examined the plaintiff in the accident and emergency department. The girl was heard first. She admitted to drinking a lot of alcohol and not remembering clearly what happened. But she did insist that she woke up the next morning with the accused in bed with her. She assumed she had been raped. When the examining doctor took the stand, it became clear that her examination of the victim was inadequate. When it was my turn to take the stand, I had to agree that the evidence for rape was lacking. The charge was therefore dropped.

I had given the examining doctor a lift to the district court. On the return journey, I felt obliged to give her some advice about improving the quality of examinations of rape victims in the future.

There was one occasion when a mother wanted to discuss the possibility that a neighbour had interfered with her daughter. The girl was aged about 10 and the neighbour was a big, burly man in his fifties. The mother seemed unsure of her story, and I was not permitted to see the little girl. I suggested that she contact the police if there was any evidence at all of an inappropriate contact. The mother backed down and apologised for bothering me.

I wondered why there was a change in the mother's attitude. If she wanted to pursue the matter any further, she should see me again or contact the police directly. I bade goodbye. As I opened the door for her onto the street I understood her change of heart. Across the road was Woolies variety store and on its flat roof was a car park. We could not mistake the appearance of the hulk of a man peering over the parapet. It was the very man the mother spoke of. He retreated when he knew we had noticed him, and she made a hasty departure. I saw neither of them again.

What can one say about all this? How should a doctor react? When he is closely involved he will naturally have an opinion. As with all his patients and as with all their problems his first and foremost response must be to listen. His purpose is not to pass judgment. That is a matter for the appropriate authority. His responsibility is to develop genuine empathy. That was needed most of all with the 16-year-old who had a stillbirth and buried her baby in the garden. It can be emotionally draining when caring for such a patient. That is especially so when information about the case must be kept confidential. In that instant, there may be no one else to share the emotional burden. But the Christian is reminded of the apostle Peter's injunction, 'Cast all your anxiety on him (God), because he cares for you.'

When dealing with misfortunes and possible crimes, one is reminded of one's own mortality and weaknesses. Indeed 'There but for the grace of God go I.' This declaration, uttered by a John Bradford before the execution of a group of prisoners in the sixteenth century has its origins in the writings of the apostle Paul. It is always wise not to assume a superior attitude. Jesus was frequently confronted by those who were self-righteous, particularly many of the Pharisees. On one occasion, he was asked about some Galileans who died at the hands of the Roman governor, Pilate. And he was asked about 18 who were killed when a tower fell on them. The implication was that the questioners assumed that those victims were being punished for their sins. Jesus' answer was, 'Do you think they were worse sinners? No, I tell you: But unless you repent, you will all perish just as they did.'[2] Jesus did not mince his words. The gospel records show that he was consistently severe with all those who were self-righteous, opinionated and hypocritical. That is because such people have rejected the need for God in their lives and without God they face a terrible judgement.

However Jesus' severe pronouncement is immediately followed by a parable illustrating God the Father's loving patience with his children.[10] The Father longs for everyone

---

[10] Luke 13: 6–9

to repent so that they can return to "life in all its fullness"[11] and a wonderful relationship with Him.

In retirement, I have had the privilege of taking part in the Kairos prison ministry. This has been an eye-opener. Men have come to our course in basic Christian living and subsequent meetings seeking a new life. There are very few men in gaol who can be described as "pure evil". The majority have suffered in many and varied ways. Many have been abused as children. On one occasion, five out of the six men on my discussion table volunteered that they had been abused by their own fathers. A large number have been introduced at a young and impressionable age to alcohol and other drugs. They have developed addictions which are always hard to conquer. Alcohol addiction is a major reason for breaking parole instructions. And we have therefore seen a number of men returned to gaol. Many inmates have had a poor education and have found it hard to hold down a job. A very small number are illiterate.

One young man in his 30s was well known to us. As a child he was in my wife's Sunday school class! His father had died of a congenital disorder, and he had a 50-50 chance of carrying the faulty gene. His mother remarried and when he was released for the last time she and her new husband met him at the gate with the intention of taking them to their new home interstate. They first visited his father's grave. By then, they had had several serious arguments and he then went his own way. He slept rough the first night and knocked on our door the next morning (a Sunday) expecting some breakfast! I immediately raised the subject of his

---

[11] John 10: 10

parole arrangement interstate and said I would help him get a rail ticket to his mother's new home. But in the meantime I was due to conduct a church service in a neighbouring parish. He went with me, and I sat him down in the front pew where I could keep an eye on him. The rest of the congregation thought he was wonderful. One of his talents was to pile on the charm! After church I bought a rail ticket and he settled into the cheapest of the local motels. The next day I assisted him to get further support from Centrelink. (He had a pension for a chronic drug problem). He then went to his old GP for further methadone supplies. The next morning he should have caught the train I had booked; but instead caught a train in the opposite direction, crossing a different state border. Since then he has settled and seems to have made good.

The motto and modus operandi of Kairos is "listen, listen, love, love". We can serve these men best when we listen carefully and intentionally to what these men say. We can earn their trust when we show that we extend to them the sort of love that Jesus displays. We know that they are in gaol for a good reason and recognise that they are responsible for what they have done. But our interest is not in their crimes. It is in their reconciliation and future life. During the four-day courses the men generally respond with trust in one another and with us. They learn that God loves them and is prepared to forgive them. They respond too with forgiveness for those who have hurt them.

Our aim as physicians is for physical and mental wholeness in our patients. Our prayer as Christians is for spiritual wholeness and reconciliation with God for those the Lord graciously puts in our path.

Matters of the Heart

'You're too young!' That is certainly an arresting start to a consultation in the confines of the doctor's surgery.

Perhaps it was put a little more delicately such as, 'I do think you appear very young.' But whatever the precise wording, one conversation did begin with an expression of that anxiety. The patient sat uneasily on the other side of my desk and concern was written on her face. Her thoughts must have ranged something like this. "Does he have enough experience?" "Does he know enough?" "Can he help me with my problem?" She may have felt uncomfortable in sharing personal, sexual details with a younger man. And did she want to undergo a gynaecological examination by a man who might be young enough to be her son?

My reply? 'How old would you like me to be?' That was not what she expected to hear. But it did hint at a little humour, and it did put her at ease. Then, having divulged my precise age she was restored to complete ease. The rest of the consultation and examination continued without any further anxiety.

In the eyes of the patient, the specialist must be old enough to have enough knowledge and experience, but young enough to be abreast of all the current research and maintain manual skill and dexterity when it comes to surgery. Arguably this is no more important than in the specialty of obstetrics and gynaecology. Not only is the patient putting her life, with all its vicissitudes, into his hands; but approximately 50% of women who cross the consulting room threshold are also expecting a new-born child. In that instance, she is committing him with a double responsibility. She expects no physical, mental or emotional harm to come to herself. She also expects to give birth to a perfect, healthy baby.

Some women express anxiety about seeing a male gynaecologist. That number was and is surprisingly few. There are now many more female gynaecologists than there were 30 or 40 years ago. A few women still prefer to see a male specialist. That group may like to feel comfortable with a father figure. Possibly a few feel that a man is more knowledgeable and skilful even though that is not the case. Nevertheless a woman seeing a male gynaecologist can pose problems.

Some patients did not easily understand what was expected of them. One was a lady who came in early in her first pregnancy. While I went to test the obligatory specimen in an adjoining room, I had invited the lady to make herself comfortable on the couch prior to an examination. On my return to the consulting room, I was greeted with a most extraordinary sight. Instead of expecting to find the lady relaxed on the couch and covered with a sheet I beheld a naked figure prancing around the room. She had evidently removed every thread of clothing and appeared to be performing some ritual dance. Fortunately, she was quiet about it. I therefore had no fears that anyone else would be wondering what was going on in doctor B's consulting room. She was not alarmed or distressed in any way. In fact, her demeanour appeared to be one of gay abandon. Perhaps she expected me to join her in some sort of jolly celebration to mark the beginning of her pregnancy? That temptation hardly registered and I managed to re-establish the required decorum and persuaded the lady to assume a dignified position on the couch with appropriate covering.

I must add that the sight of the naked body was not a pretty one. In my experience of meeting about 50,000 female patients, I have concluded that a good set of clothes definitely enhances attractiveness.

Many years ago a coterie of attractive young ladies used to come to the surgery on the same day. They were expecting babies and therefore came for antenatal check-ups. My wife said they came on "lovely lady day". I admired them all. I have to say that I feel genuine beauty resides even more in the person's character.

One of my chief mentors during my specialist training was a beautiful lady. She held a senior position in the Royal College of Obstetricians and Gynaecologists in London where she examined new specialist aspirants. There were very few lady gynaecologists at the time, and it was exceptionally rare for a married woman with a family, as she had, to become a specialist in any medical field. As well as being an exceptional physician and surgeon she was also an astute psychologist. Incidentally, she was also a magistrate in the children's court. Her vast experience in medicine as well as motherhood made her eminently qualified to pass on her wisdom. She held what came to be called her "serenity" talks. As part of the antenatal classes she taught the expectant mothers how to maintain confidence, poise and attractiveness through the pregnancy and into the postnatal period. One most important piece of advice she passed to us, the trainee specialists, was never open your mouth until you have something helpful to say. The patient will not be helped with platitudes, and it is better to say nothing than to spout a dubious truth, however encouraging that might seem to be.

Another of my young patients quickly earned the nickname "Puss in Boots". She was given this name unanimously by the receptionists and clerical staff. She was petite and still a teenager. Her boots came up to mid-thigh and her shorts could not have been shorter. She was one who was keen to make a statement and demonstrate her own idea of attractiveness.

One had to be prepared for a variety of mental and emotional responses. Abuse was reported from time to time. I was even asked to assist with a case of domestic violence. Listening and responding appropriately requires special concentration. One lady could not sit on the patient's chair to tell her story. Instead she insisted that she lie on the floor for the duration of the interview. All the while she fanned herself with a particularly elaborate fan. It was not hot at the time, and I later discovered that she also performed her protracted histrionics in other doctors' rooms also. Another lady carried a large, pressurised spray can which she used liberally and repeatedly on herself during her consultation.

One lady aged in her 50s returned for a check-up. She and her husband had recently terminated an unhappy marriage and she moved over 100 kms away to start a new life. In her new environment, she met Mr Wonderful. On her return, she was eager to tell me about her new beau and was even more eager to relate her sexual encounters with him. She claimed to have experienced 52 orgasms in three weeks!

At that time, we rented one of a row of three shopfronts built by a friend who was a nurseryman. He used one for his produce and the third was a hairdresser's. The complex was known as the three "Ps", pills, perms and plants! Our suite had three rooms. The front room was the waiting area which included the receptionist's desk. The back room was for storage and general utility and was connected to the front by a narrow corridor. The only windows were at the front and back of the building. The central consulting room, therefore, had no windows and ventilation was afforded by a 30 cms space at the top of the three internal walls. Sound proofing was therefore non-existent.

The sexual experience with Mr Wonderful was related in explicit detail. My patient's voice rose decibel by decibel as she relived the sheer ecstasy. She had abundant breasts and as she became more and more excited the breasts heaved up and down. I wondered if the bra would hold or whether the ample bosom would at any moment escape from its mooring. My mind conjured up the expressions on the faces of those in the waiting area. All too late I had wished for there to be a radio to compete with my patient's lurid story. I imagined mothers placing their hands firmly over their daughters' ears. All I could do was put my finger to my mouth and utter, 'Sh, sh, ssh, ssshhh.' She took no notice of my protestations. She was determined to conclude the narrative, and nothing would interrupt her.

A more worrying conversation involved a young lady in her early twenties. I had escorted her from the waiting room to her chair in front of my desk. She had barely given me time to resume my seat when she blurted out, 'Do you find me attractive?' That came like a bolt out of the blue. It required immediate analysis and a considered response.

The incident occurred in a consulting room with very good sound proofing. There was no natural light. It was usual for most patients to come into the room on their own. But if a patient was nervous or very young or incapacitated I would ask the receptionist to act as a chaperone. This particular young lady came in at the start of the consultation by herself.

What prompted her question? Was she making a sexual advance? I would have been about twice her age. The thought of a romantic attachment was furthest from my mind. As it happens gynaecologists are statistically much less likely to fall into this temptation than other specialists. For understandable reasons, it is the psychiatrists who are most likely, and they are followed, according to one survey, by ENT surgeons and skin specialists.

Perhaps it was a genuine question prompted by low self-esteem. Perhaps she had been rejected by a boyfriend. The correct response to any question from a patient is one of empathy. One always takes the question at face value. If there is any malicious intent hidden in the patient's agenda, it will be clearly evident as the conversation progresses. I was once threatened by a patient who the police informed me had a knife and a firearm, both of which she was determined to use. In this instance, the police were concerned for my safety. She suffered from a poorly controlled mental affliction and previous conversations certainly smacked of malicious intent.

In the case of the young lady, I did assure her that she was not unattractive. I then switched immediately to the matter in hand and told her she had consulted me for a medical reason. She had come to see me as her gynaecologist. It is not easy to analyse the mind of a young lady after the utterance of just one sentence. But one is always assisted by body language. In fact, the body language, particularly in this instance, says oceans more than the spoken word.

Having established a proper relationship I invited her to express any fears and concerns she might have. This gave her leave to talk about issues that might not be related to the medical reason she presented with. When we had concluded the conversation, I recommended that we invite the receptionist to be present for the examination. The consultation ended on an amicable note.

Conversations in the consulting room were never boring. On the contrary, there was often an interesting tale attached to the medical problem. Patients came from differing backgrounds. Many were born overseas. Amongst the varieties of different nationalities every country in Europe except Albania was represented. Most of the countries in the Americas, SE Asia and the Pacific as well as many African countries were represented by some colourful ambassadors gracing my rooms.

Some will go to extraordinary lengths to satisfy their husbands' demands. Mrs X was sent home after the insertion of a suture into the neck of her womb. She had suffered late miscarriages indicating a weakness in that area. Later in the evening we were entertaining two other doctors and their wives to dinner. At about 9.00 p.m., the phone rang. It was

Mrs X's neighbour. Mrs X had sent her to the phone box down her road. The message was: "Mrs X wants to know can she have her relations?" Our dinner guests could hardly contain themselves when I repeated the conversation. I had apparently not included the obvious when I discharged the lady from the hospital. She most certainly should not have her "relations", not that night and not for next few weeks.

Good communication, particularly with post-operative instructions, is an essential feature of patient care. In that case, I failed, but all was well for the rest of the pregnancy.

Passing on accurate, timely and easily understood information is only one aspect of a good doctor to patient relationship. For a male gynaecologist, there is a definite period of learning before the doctor is really comfortable with the relationship. As the cases I have described illustrate there must be constant attention to a professional approach. It may be perfectly appropriate for a patient to express the emotional aspects of her complaint. But her medical attendant's reaction must be one of unemotional empathy.

With the exception of psychiatrists, all doctors will tend to concentrate on the physical needs of their patients. A general practitioner may address their emotional needs as well; but specialists will generally consider that to be someone else's problem. In the "good old days", we did not have the luxury of assistance from psychologists and counsellors. Consequently it was up to us to tackle the social and emotional problems as best we could. In obstetrics and gynaecology in particular, there is a need to take a holistic approach. For a male specialist, it became apparent that one must learn some basic psychological skills as quickly as possible.

When considering how a male doctor should relate to female patients, one cannot do better than look at the example of Jesus. The Gospel records contain many examples of His dealings with women. One of the best known is His encounter with a woman who was caught in the very act of adultery[12]. The scribes and Pharisees maintained that according to Mosaic Law she should be stoned. 'What do you say?' they demanded. But instead of answering immediately Jesus bent down and wrote with his finger on the ground. To me this is the most important point of the story. Jesus was carefully listening; He was carefully observing; he was waiting for the grumbling and murmuring to settle down. Like my esteemed lady mentor He was waiting for the right moment to speak. He waited for the moment when the emotions had settled, and his words would be clearly understood. And when he did speak it was something really profound. He had to answer the woman's accusers and minister to the woman herself. When he had their full attention He regaled the scribes and Pharisees by saying that only someone totally without sin could carry out the judgement. That meant of course that He was the only man who met those stipulations. The accusers slunk away, and Jesus could then minister to the woman alone. He spoke tenderly to her and directed her towards a wholesome way of life.

That incident teaches us to be patient, to listen very carefully and only open our mouths when we have something worth saying. Everything we do say must be said in an attitude of genuine empathy.

---

[12] John 8: 3–11

A similar encounter occurred at a dinner party with Simon the Pharisee.[13] During the meal a woman bursts in and as an act of sheer devotion washes Jesus' feet with her tears and then anoints them with expensive ointment. Most likely Jesus had met her previously and had helped her change her lifestyle. The story implies that the woman was a prostitute, and it ends with Jesus reiterating the forgiveness the woman desperately needed.

It is so easy to be judgemental. As these two accounts illustrate the right response is to give advice with empathy and understanding. Also it is so easy to show shock when confronted with evidence of sexual perversion. I well remember having to repair a genital laceration which was bleeding heavily. The young lady would not say anything to indicate how she received the injury. My duty was to show tenderness. An interrogation was definitely not appropriate.

Finally it was on the cross of Calvary when Jesus expressed His most tender moment.[14] He was acutely aware of His mother's distress as she watched His life draining away in that most cruel and barbaric way. Even as He suffered excruciating physical and emotional pain He was able to concentrate on the needs of others, particularly His nearest and dearest. He directed that His disciple John should care for His mother and develop a new mother and son relationship.

---

[13] Luke 7: 36–50
[14] John 19: 25–27

Shalom

It was the famous essayist, Francis Bacon, who, almost 400 years ago wrote that travel is part of education[15]. Although he had it in mind for the traveller to inspect important monuments, I have maintained that it is a privilege and more valuable to meet and be entertained by the local people. To become immersed in a foreign culture is a true education. To understand the burdens of the poorest people on earth is an even greater education and invokes a massive challenge.

In 1996, I had the opportunity to visit Ethiopia for the first time. Our son, Andrew, had spent his elective term in medical training at Murgwanza Hospital in far Northwest Tanzania. He developed a burning desire to devote his life's work to the care of poor women in East Africa. His aunt Valerie, my sister, had settled in the Afar region of Ethiopia. After completing nursing training at the Children's Hospital in Sydney, she and a friend travelled to Ethiopia in 1973. There they cared for many children stricken by the effects of one of the worst famines in that country's history. Valerie was "bitten by the African bug" and returned to Ethiopia

---

[15] John Pilcher "The Essays" (Harmondsworth Penguin 1985) In the Penguin Classics series.

many times till in 1989 she married an Afar, Ismael, and settled permanently in that land.

The Afar is one the defined regions of Ethiopia with its own regional government. It lies in the Great Rift Valley and includes the Danakil depression and eight active volcanoes. The area is about 900 kms from North to South and 300 kms at its widest. The Afar people are mainly nomads. They have a rich oral history going back to the time of the Pharaohs. For political and geographical reasons, they have enjoyed very little support from the central government. Valerie has always wanted to help the underdog and in 1993 she and Ismael founded an indigenous NGO, the Afar Pastoralist Development Association, which now supports 1.5 million people.[16]

Andrew wanted to visit his aunt and find out what he possibly could do to help her. He was also determined to visit Dr Catherine Hamlin and her fistula hospital. I was eager to accompany him and would find the experience one which gave me long lasting insight into the needs and burdens of the unprivileged. I would be deeply humbled.

We travelled separately to Cairo. From there, we completed our journey from Australia together. We left Egypt in darkness and as dawn broke we could see the mountains of Ethiopia. As we descended the attractive countryside came into view. There was a patchwork of different colours produced by the variety of crops in the multitude of tiny paddocks. The impression was one of

---

[16] "Maalika – my life among the Afar nomads of Africa". Valerie Browning and John Little – Pan Macmillan – 2008

productivity, beauty and peace. That was contrary to the human turmoil we would soon encounter.

We landed at the capital, Addis Ababa. In 1996, its population numbered four million. There are many more now and in the whole country there are now about 100 million souls. The airport in 1996 was insignificant, unlike the big modern airport of today. It reminded me then of Armidale in regional NSW. The welcomers were leaning over a wire fence. We easily spotted Valerie and her daughter, Aisha, five years old.

A friend had supplied a "Ute" to meet us. The journey to Valerie's house on the Eastern side of the city was not a comfortable one. The "Ute" was not in good working order: The roads were full of potholes and progress was slow because of the four-legged traffic on the road, sheep, goats and donkeys.

There was a tremendous welcome in Valerie's house. Afar girls prepared a coffee ceremony. This is a universal mark of hospitality in Ethiopia. Green beans were roasted in a small, heavy pan over a charcoal brazier. When the roasting was complete, the pan was passed around for every guest to savour the aroma at close quarters. Then the beans were ground with mortar and pestle. A second brazier was heating water to boiling point in a traditional coffee pot. The coffee grounds were added, and the strong coffee was poured into tiny cups without handles. We were expected to drink three cups with mountains of sugar.

The coffee ceremony set the tone for genuine friendship. The assembly was mostly Afar. One young man, Abdullah, was an amputee. He had suffered serious gunshot wounds resulting in osteomyelitis. This necessitated amputation of

74

his leg above the knee. Another man, Ismael "Rusta" was very talkative. He was one who spoke a lot of English. He had developed what must have been post-traumatic stress after fighting in the war in Djibouti. He was very keen to let us know that Valerie is known as Maalika, the mother of the Afar.[2]

It soon became clear that about 20 people slept at Valerie's home each night. Valerie later explained that her husband, Ismael, did not collect postage stamps or trinkets as other men did: he collected people. He felt sorry for the homeless, the destitute and the injured. He would invite them to stay. The house was solid, made of stone with an iron roof. The floor was concrete and there were no floor coverings. Every square inch of the living room accommodated sleeping mats. There was one bedroom and a kitchen. There was also a small outhouse. The girls slept there, and the men slept in the main house. There was one bed and no other furniture of any significance. Being the honoured guest and the oldest person present it would have been very bad form if I refused the offer of the bed.

I had my 56th birthday in Ethiopia. The average life expectancy for women was 50 and for men only a little more.

There was concern in the city about further terrorism following bombing of hotels. We went to a bank to cash travellers' cheques. At the door, we were greeted by armed guards. Our cameras were left in the care of the guards, and we were body-searched. Bank cards had not been introduced to Ethiopia. There was a long process involving at least three bank clerks before we were the proud owners of Ethiopian currency. We also went to buy postage stamps. At the post office, there were more armed guards. We were body searched again and relieved temporarily of our cameras.

It was not clear who was responsible for the bombing. It was probably Somalis. There has been recurrent conflict between the two countries. Ownership of land in the Ogaden desert region is disputed. But there is also internal political tension. The communist regime in Ethiopia came to an end in 1991 and there is supposed to be a democratic government in place. There are three main highland groups which comprise the lion's share of the total population.

The Amharas, to whom belonged the emperors Haile Selassie and Menilek, were in power for many decades, if not centuries.

The Tigrays, the smallest of the three highland groups, have held power from 1991. Each general election was marked by protests against unfairness in the process. All those who objected to the rigging of the elections were imprisoned, or worse. When I was there in 2008, Amnesty International estimated that about 40,000 people were in gaol. Those in power targeted the intellectuals in particular. There are many well educated Ethiopians who are teachers, lawyers and journalists.

In 2019, there was a minor miracle. The last Tigray prime minister died suddenly of a heart attack. He was replaced by an Oromo who is also a protestant Christian. The Oromo are the largest of the highland groups, numbering about 30 million. The new prime minister has indicated that he wants to exercise more inclusive government. He has been awarded a Nobel peace prize for his part in bringing the long-standing war with Eritrea to a close. Unhappily, the old guard are still active, and the new

PM has had threats to his life. Beginning in 2020 there has been further bloodshed. A Tigray insurgency has sought to regain power. They have been well armed, and the larger federal force has not found it easy to quell the uprising. There have been thousands of deaths and many more have fled for shelter in the Sudan and into the Afar region of Ethiopia.

While we did our business in the bank and post office, the Afar girls at Valerie's house were preparing for a party. About 100 were invited to farewell a group of refugees. These were all young men who had been involved in the fighting in Djibouti. They had mostly lost close family members. They were deemed persona non grata in the jurisdictions of Djibouti, Eritrea and Ethiopia. The old French colony of Djibouti is now the Democratic Republic of the Afar and the Issar. The Issar are related to the Somalis and in Djibouti they outnumbered the Afar. The fighting spilled over into Eritrea and Ethiopia. These young men had stood up to an enemy which was dispossessing them of land and livestock.

The US had accepted the current group of refugees. They were to fly via Frankfurt that very evening. There had been a lot of frantic work the night before. Valerie had spent the wee small hours preparing papers for them, working urgently on her typewriter.

For the party, a large number of chairs were borrowed, comfortable chairs for the lounge room and stackable chairs for the patio outside. The house, like others in the street, sat on a small block of less than ¼ acre. However the majority of homes in the area were mudbrick and occupied by large families. Valerie's rented home was bordered by a high stone wall. The only entrance was via a high iron gate which was locked at night. The wall was hidden on the inside by a high hedge. A small veranda outside the front door was covered with large wooden crates containing grinding equipment waiting to be shipped to the Afar region.

It was most interesting to meet some Europeans amongst the invited guests. There was a French teacher from the lycée in the city. There were three young people from the USA who had degrees in anthropology. They were studying the local culture. Dr Enid Parker and Margaret Munro had come out from England for two months. They had both served in the Red Sea Mission Team, Dr Enid for 40 years and Margaret for a somewhat shorter period. The Red Sea Mission Team is a fairly small Christian mission. Its motto is "Islam shall hear". Their area of service includes the Yemen, Eritrea and Djibouti. (The gentleman I met on the steps of Guy's hospital in 1960 was a leading member of the Team). Dr Enid has recorded her work in a handsome book.[17] In 1996, she was just over 70 and looked a little frail. She had pioneered literacy for the Afar and was anxious to know what progress had been made. Her mission group in London, who had taken responsibility for her welfare, had forbidden her from travelling into the inhospitable Afar region at her age. Margaret did, however, accompany us.

Just beyond the patio was a small area of grass, which was the chosen spot for the traditional Afar dancing. This consisted of only one couple dancing at a time. The others marked the rhythm with clapping. One man played a small

---

[17] "My Life Among the Afar People" – 2014 – ISBN – 978-1-291-86189-1

drum. There was lusty singing, a lot of tunes being contemporary European songs.

The time came for the men to be taken to the airport. One young man had obvious mixed feelings. Like the others he had never been out of the country before. He had certainly never travelled by air. He faced an unknown future. He did not know whether he was doing the right thing. But if he stayed he could easily be killed. He desperately needed reassurance. So he sought blessings from the elders. He came first to me. That was a tremendous honour. As someone who had only just met him and as someone who had no knowledge whatsoever of his language the cultural gulf was huge. But it was immediately apparent that as Valerie's older brother (I am almost ten years her senior) I had earned his immediate respect. The young man obviously expected a warm embrace and words expressing the favour of almighty God. These I gave without hesitation. I think someone must have translated my English. It was a most moving experience and one I shall never forget.

After we returned from our journey into the Afar region two weeks later, we were amazed and delighted to receive good news from USA. All of the refugees had found jobs. The process of settling into a new land and a new culture had got off to a fine start.

The day after the party was a Sunday and it was only our second full day in Ethiopia. Early in the morning Andrew and I climbed the hill behind Val's house. First we traversed some winding dirt tracks which were lined by overcrowded mud brick homes. We were met by laughing children eager to warn us of the "hyena stone house". Evidently some hyenas lived in caves on the top of the hill a few hundred metres above the city. On the slopes were goats and cattle grazing under the watchful eyes of herdsmen.

The view from the top of the hill was worth the climb. The city was spread out below us. It nestles in rolling hills. It was founded in the nineteenth century and the Empress named it "beautiful flower". That translates to Addis Ababa. The hills attract a good rainfall, most of the time. It boasts a very pleasant climate, being at 8000 feet above sea level and just nine degrees north of the equator.

Val, Aicha, Andrew and I made our way by minicab to the International Evangelical church for the morning service. It is housed in a modern building and seats about 1000 people. Behind it is a courtyard surrounded by rooms where groups met for Bible studies. The majority of the congregation were Ethiopian. Among the whites there was a fair sprinkling of Americans. Val had a dark friend who was crippled by polio. She always sat near the front. To join her was a little embarrassing because we had arrived late.

Val had a white Australian friend named Andy who was in the same Bible study group. Andy was married to an Ethiopian lady, and they had young children. He worked for Tearfund Australia. The previous day we had heard the very disturbing news that an Ethiopian airline plane had been hijacked. It was on a routine flight from Addis Ababa to Nairobi and Andy was one of the passengers.

The armed hijacker demanded to be taken to Australia. With the news of a hijacker on board landing at Nairobi was forbidden. The plane could not therefore take on more fuel. In 1996, access to the cockpit was easy and the armed man constantly harassed the pilot. He was forced to head towards Australia and so prepared for a watery landing. The fuel load was almost exhausted as the plane approached the Comoros Islands. The pilot was well trained: Ethiopian airlines had expert instruction from Lufthansa. As the plane descended the pilot chose the calmest water near the shore. But the hijacker disturbed his concentration. The plane hit a rock and overturned.

A tourist on the island captured the landing on video and the recording was posted around the world. The world then knew about the tragedy but knew nothing of reports we later received.

There were 175 passengers and crew on board that plane. Only 50 survived. Andy was one of the casualties. Reports came back eventually to family members in Ethiopia. Survivors said that Andy had shared the Gospel and 20 had gladly received Christ as their Lord and Saviour. The cabin was then filled with the sound of joyful Christian songs!

Back in Bowral, some months later, I received two visitors from Melbourne. One was an Afar accountant. He had settled in Australia about ten years previously and had become well established in his profession. There is quite a large group of Afar in Melbourne. The Afar diaspora are fewer in number in Sydney; but there are larger groups in New Zealand and Sweden. The accountant brought with him a refugee from the Afar who was seeking a protection visa. Like the young men I met at Valerie's house he had been fighting in the war in Djibouti. And like them he was persona non grata in Djibouti, Eritrea and Ethiopia. His life would have been in danger had he stayed.

Hayden – I will call him that because that is how his name transliterated – Hayden had borrowed a passport and travelled to Australia by air via Cairo. He needed some evidence that he was fleeing a genuine life-threatening situation. Because I had recently travelled in the Afar region and was acquainted with the political situation it was assumed a letter from me to the department of immigration might carry some weight.

The two men walked up from the railway station in Bowral and met me in my surgery. They sat opposite me in my consulting room. At once, I could see that Hayden was a picture of anxiety. His brow was furrowed, and his darting eyes gave the appearance of urgent searching. Would I help? Would he be allowed to stay in Australia? And what about his loved ones he had left behind in Ethiopia? The accountant relayed Hayden's story and I confirmed what I knew of the war from which he had escaped. It was agreed I could write to the Immigration department. While we spoke, the evidence of anxiety on Hayden's face continued. He spoke no English and understood nothing of what we were saying.

It came time to walk back to the railway station. I accompanied them both. I searched for something meaningful to say as we bade farewell. I could only manage two words in Afar; but I did remember the Arabic greeting. Almost all the Afar are Muslims and so they would know it. 'Al-salam alaikum!' What a transformation! As I uttered those words all signs of anxiety melted. Instead there was the most beautiful and broadest smile I had ever seen.

Not long after that encounter I was given the opportunity to relate the details of Hayden's story and the meaning of the Arab greeting to an assembly at a local high school. At the end of the assembly, it was a Muslim boy who broke ranks and rushed up to thank me for what I had just said.

The Arabic greeting, "Al-salam 'alaikum" is the same as the Hebrew "shalom alechem". It is the greeting our Lord Jesus gave to his disciples in the upper room after His resurrection. In English, it is translated, 'Peace be with you.'[18] But in English we do not have a word which adequately fulfils the meaning of the Hebrew or Arabic. "Shalom" means much more than a wish for the absence of conflict. It is a wish, a prayer, for the total wellbeing in the person being addressed. For the Christian, and indeed for the Jew and the Muslim, it means, especially, spiritual wellbeing, peace with God. In that upper room, Jesus met with His disciples who were all frightened: They were scared the Jewish authorities would arrest them. Jesus's presence and His greeting was just what they needed.

The apostle Paul always began his letters with the greeting: 'Grace to you and peace.'[19] The grace of our Lord Jesus Christ is the means and peace is the result.

Hayden hungered for the peace which would fill his heart with hope. The young man who came for my blessing craved peace before he embarked on a journey into the unknown. Andy's widow and young children would long for the peace which would quieten the pain of bereavement. In every case, Jesus is the source of that peace.

---

[18] John 20: 19 New Revised Standard Version
[19] Romans 1: 7 and the beginnings of the other letters of the Apostle Paul

The Word

Following our arrival in Valerie's house, the farewell party for the refugees and the visit to the international church preparations were made over the next two days for our epic journey into the Afar. The needs of those people are enormous. By any standard, they must be one of the most underprivileged groups on earth. In 1996, the UN ranked Ethiopia as the poorest nation on earth. The Afar are still the poorest of the poor. As nomads they do not own land. What little wealth they have rests entirely with their livestock. The livestock, in turn, are reliant on the land and the rainfall to provide pasture.

Poverty can neatly be defined by annual income relative to the cost of living. But that ignores the most important aspect of poverty. No one can lift their standard of living unless they have a voice that is heard. In the case of the Afar, much of their most productive land was taken over by the highlanders, mainly Amharas. Valerie defines poverty as voicelessness – the fact that the Afar have no effective representation. Individuals might dare to speak, but if no one in authority is prepared to listen they would continue in their parlous state.

In 2000, the UN promulgated the millennium development goals to alleviate poverty in all its guises. The UN emphasised literacy as of prime importance. Valerie had realised this years earlier. She was determined that the first major program of the Afar Pastoral Development Association would be literacy. When many more of the Afar were educated, they could make effective representations to the federal government. They could also interact more positively with the highland groups, both commercially and socially.

Even before rising to the educational standards of the highlanders some surprising friendships developed. Two days after our arrival in Ethiopia Valerie had an invitation to afternoon tea from Footsum who had been a genuine friend since Valerie had lived in that part of town. She was an Amhara and Valerie could not understand why she had been so kind to her Afar household. The Amhara often despise the Afar; but Footsum's approach seemed like genuine, selfless love.

Footsum lived in the street below Valerie's house. Her home was constructed of mud, iron and timber. It was jammed tight against similar dwellings on each side. Inside it was relatively comfortable. We were shown into a living room which measured about $3 \times 2^{1}/_{2}$ metres. There were a few scattered pieces of wallpaper clinging tastefully to the walls and furniture for three to sit comfortably. Two charcoal braziers were on the floor in the centre of the room and the coffee ceremony began.

Only one person in the room apart from Andrew and I spoke English. He was a Tigray man, a highlander, named Tgasey. He had been a truck driver and had fallen on hard times. Ismael had taken him in and provided hospitality. Tgasey was unique in that he was the only man I saw in Ethiopia who had a generous covering to his belly. There must have been a time when he was relatively well off. The only woman I saw in that category was sitting in a Mercedes! Everyone else was slim and many were obviously malnourished.

We later learnt that Tgasey became very useful to Valerie and Ismael helping to transport their stores. He has been introduced to the Gospel and has responded to the invitation of the Lord Jesus.

While the coffee beans were being roasted, Tgasey was very keen to explain to me what was going on. He was also keen to provide me with some of the local brew. He fetched a sample; but I decided it had a distinct resemblance to sump oil! Apparently it was made from rotting bananas. Tgasey spotted my disapproval and went out again. He returned with a look of glee on his face and poured two glasses of neat spirit.

Meanwhile Footsum was treating us royally. The beautiful aroma of freshly brewed coffee permeated the room. This was augmented by handfuls of frankincense being put onto the braziers. We all consumed the traditional three tiny cups of coffee. The whole atmosphere was one of generous hospitality in spite of obvious poverty. In the absence of ready communication, it is generous hospitality which speaks volumes of unuttered words.

Before leaving on our journey to the Afar, there was some shopping to be done. We needed to purchase exercise books and other essentials for the literacy classes. A Toyota Landcruiser was hired from Oxfam. We learnt that this was a luxury for Valerie. She usually thumbed a lift with a truck driver. Drivers took as many people as they could squeeze into their cab and charged a reasonable rate. Safety was not a priority, and the accident rate was horrendous.

The Landcruiser came with an Oxfam driver, Daniel who was an Amhara. It turned out that Daniel had little experience of driving in the remote parts of the country and may never have been off the highway into Afar territory. Initially we were eight in the vehicle, including Margaret Munro whom we collected from the SIM building in town (Serving in Mission and previously the Sudan Interior Mission). We carried a lot of gear besides our personal belongings. This included two large boxes full of kits for the bush nurses, which were supplied by WHO.

Dr Enid Parker saw us off with a very sincere prayer. She had wanted to travel with us but neither we nor her church wanted to be responsible for her in the Afar on account of her mild frailty.

Dr Enid had pioneered literacy for the Afar. In her 40 years of service with them, she had studied their oral language. She had identified 17 vowel sounds and eventually put their oral language into written form. Thanks to Enid theirs is the only language in Ethiopia which employs the Roman script. Its origins are Cushitic which is quite different from the highland Semitic languages. Enid gained a PhD from London University for this work. In 1985, she, with one other linguist, published an Afar, English-French dictionary with London University's School of Oriental and African Studies. An Afar called Omar had been educated at Heidelberg University. He was very keen for me to have a copy of the dictionary and gave me one for my birthday which fell on a day when we returned to Addis Ababa. Enid was passionate about the need for literacy. In her book, "My life among the Afar People" she wrote, 'The people who invest time and energy into the study and recording of their own language can become strong. Otherwise they become servants of other groups who do.'[20] Valerie would add that without literacy the people would be completely at the mercy of those who seek to take advantage of them.

Our first night after leaving Addis Ababa was spent at the George Inn in Awash which is by the river of the same name. It was only 225 kms from Addis. It marked the beginning of Afar territory, and we had already descended several thousand feet. On the way, we passed through Nazret which is quite a large industrial town. The rooms in the Inn were luxurious compared with hostelry further on. Half of them had their own en suites and we paid about $4 each for the night.

The next morning we left early and soon drove off the bitumen highway. On a dirt road, a bus coming towards us stopped. A man got out and joined us. It never ceased to amaze me how many friendly contacts Valerie has, scattered over a very wide area.

We continued our journey through farming land and came suddenly upon a village called Citygafargi. We made our way to a hotel for breakfast. This was served in an Ethiopian style gazebo in the forecourt. Then we met Ibrahim. He was a local Afar literacy co-ordinator. His whole manner conveyed his passion for the work. He was

---

[20] My life Among the Afar People. Enid M Parker 2014 ISBN 978-1-291-861189-1 page 137

oozing with enthusiasm and was delighted to receive the primers from Margaret.

With breakfast completed, we went for a walk through the centre of the village with its quaint shops and small timber buildings lining narrow streets. Andrew, Margaret and I were the objects of curiosity rather than the source of ready cash. That made a nice change! At one point Aisha, who was naturally gregarious, made friends with a boy about the same age, which is five. They walked together hand in hand in front of us. Aisha was proudly carrying a little school case, a present we brought out from a friend in Australia.

We drove to the edge of the village where we found the local high school which accommodates 850 students. We met with the principal who came across as a very understanding man. I thought he explained his school's limitations very well and handled the abrasive Valerie very graciously. Valerie wanted to know why the Afar language was not being taught even though the school was in Afar territory. The Amharas from the highlands have taken over the commercial interests in the Rift Valley and run the schools.

We were taken to a class where public health was being taught. We noticed that all the students were spontaneously polite and attentive. It appeared that there were no problems with discipline and that the students were keen to learn.

We noticed that the school's national flag was flying at half-mast. The tragic news of the hijacked aircraft and its ditching in the Indian Ocean had obviously reached them. That occurred three days earlier. The whole country was in mourning.

Not far from the school we were shewn a banana plantation. We were told that it occupied 800 hectares and was therefore a large enterprise, run of course by Amharas. We were invited to load bananas into any vacant place we could find in the Landcruiser. As we were leaving Daniel, the driver, spotted a dung beetle crossing the dirt track in front of us. I was accused of acting like a Japanese tourist as I jumped out for the obligatory photo. The beetle was proudly rolling a ball of dung several times his own size.

Back on the bitumen highway Daniel put his foot down. I glimpsed the speedo a few times and it was nudging 120 kms/hour on some straight stretches. It was on one such stretch that there was a massive explosion. The vehicle lurched menacingly from side to side. Daniel brought it safely to a halt. A rear tyre had burst. We were very grateful that it wasn't a front tyre. In that instance, the Landcruiser would not have remained upright. Changing the wheel was a challenge. I was alarmed to find that there was not an adequate supply of tools on board. The spare wheel was difficult to dislodge from its housing and I found my Swiss army knife and pocket torch very useful.

The state of the highway was a great concern. Vehicles, even heavy trucks, would travel at high speed on the wrong side of the road to avoid potholes. Serious accidents were evidently common judging by the number of overturned trucks on the side of the road. Big trucks, we were told, would take three days to travel the 884 kms from Addis Ababa to Assab on the coast of Eritrea. The road surface is good near Addis, poor near the coast and mediocre in between. When relations with Eritrea worsened and the border was closed, Ethiopia turned to Djibouti as its lifeline with the outside world. That made the whole journey just a little longer.

On a dirt section of the highway, we came across an Afar community camped by the roadside and selling matting to passers-by. At this point, we met a fully armed Afar man for the first time. He carried the traditional large curved Afar knife and a Russian AK 47 semi-automatic rifle with plenty of ammunition. We turned off to a village nearby and found another man similarly armed. At this village, there were a number of sick people. Some were obviously anaemic, probably from chronic malaria. It is amazing that some Afar keep going with exceptionally low haemoglobin levels. (Haemoglobin is the oxygen carrying chemical in red blood cells). Levels even as low as one tenth the normal strength have been recorded!

Our next stop was at an agricultural training station where we hoped to replace our burst tyre. Unfortunately, none could be found. We were however treated to the sight of three traditionally dressed and armed Afar young men. At the age of five, a young boy is given a staff. At ten, he is equipped with the big, curved knife which he wears in a leather sheath on his belt. And at 15 he gets an AK47. Although in 1996 there was ammunition left over from the coup in 1991, the supply would gradually dry up. When I visited in 2008, I did not see any. Those three young men were dressed as warriors. Their hair was coated with camel fat which apparently attracts the ladies and makes them look like their equivalent of Mel Gibson.

Besides the rifles which were easy to come by other detritus of war was evident. We saw burnt out Russian tanks and army trucks lying in the countryside.

As night fell we reached "lovely" Logia. This is a town on the highway and about halfway to the coast. It is a popular truck stop. We found accommodation at St Michael's guest house. The cost was $1 Australian for one night. Andrew and I had beds in the outside passageway. This was separated by a low wooden fence from a noisy herd of goats. We had to use our own mozzie nets. The town did not have mains electricity and the hotel's generator went off at 9.00 p.m. Therefore we were advised to purchase a candle for 20 cents to light our way to the washroom and hole in the ground. Bottled water was however placed under each bed for personal use. We had had a busy day and slept well.

The next day we set off to Assaita. The town is the seat of an ancient sultanate. When we turned off the highway, the countryside was arid. The view to our right had the appearance of a scene from "Lawrence of Arabia". There were no trees. On the skyline was a caravan of camels and as the sand was heating up there was a mirage in the middle ground. Assaita had a remarkable Arabian look about it. The houses had flat roofs and the streets were very narrow, making it difficult to manoeuvre our Landcruiser. There were plenty of shops and restaurants, not five-star establishments of course, but serving wholesome food, nevertheless. There was a large dusty square in the town centre and two mosques.

We caught up with my brother-in-law, Ismael at last. He was very keen to show us a house he was renting for the all-important literacy classes. Women were flocking to the classes and by targeting the women the men were bound to follow. The Afar, particularly the younger ones, could see at once that becoming literate was vital. They understood straight away that they would then be much more able to communicate their needs and concerns as a community. Later we saw photos of classes being set up under trees. This would happen wherever the Afar were camped. The teachers were the bright young Afar themselves – men and women. The only equipment they needed was some chalk and a blackboard.

Our hotel was most unimpressive on the outside with an untidy mud wall. Inside the rooms led onto a spacious courtyard equipped with washing lines. Water was had from an old fuel tank on a stand. There was also a massive earthenware jar. This, with the buildings, was a reminder of biblical times. At the end of the courtyard, there was a vertical drop of about 100 feet to the river below.

As it was warm Andrew, and I chose to sleep on the flat roof. We were provided with mosquito nets which fitted over frames above our beds. From our vantage point, we looked over the town boundary and down to the Awash River running swiftly by. On the far side of the river, there was an Afar village comprising a group of deboitas. These are portable hemispherical shelters made of curved sticks and matting. They are about ten feet in diameter, and one is easily packed onto a camel for transport to the next grazing ground.

Just upstream on our side of the river was a large paddock of corn. Downstream the riverbank was strewn with all the refuse from the town. Scavenging were a large monitor lizard, and a squirrel-like mammal called an Oris. Flitting amongst the bushes were exquisite birds of every imaginable colour. Apparently 240 rare species inhabit the Awash valley. Scampering over the roofs were barbary apes.

The "smallest room in the house" was situated on the edge of the precipice so that the effluent would descend the cliff face. There was a constant updraft. This made the disposal of paper very difficult. The shower house next door was the home of a myriad of cockroaches. They were quite spectacular as they displayed every imaginable colour. They moved swiftly over every available surface.

We observed a beautiful sunset from our rooftop and rose early to see a great sunrise. The beauty of the sky lifted our hearts and instead of dwelling on the domestic discomforts our thoughts ranged towards eternal things. It was at this point that Margaret requested to join Andrew and me in our daily devotion and Bible reading.

We were witnessing a revolution in the minds of the Afar. Without changing their lifestyle they now had in their possession the means to advance their place in the world. In particular, they would be able to voice their desires and aspirations more effectively at the seat of power in Addis Ababa. As a smaller region in population they would have the opportunity to exercise their proportional influence in the federal government. This was made possible by the introduction of literacy. In addition to the political benefits, they also had the means to understand their Muslim faith more precisely and compare their traditional faith with Christianity.

As an example of the benefits of literacy Valerie's campaign to eradicate female genital mutilation (FGM) was made so much more effective. For thousands of years, possibly 5,000, the Afar have practised the most severe form of female genital cutting, as it is called. The origin of the practice is unclear; but the older women insist that a girl

94

cannot enter womanhood unless it is done. It is performed when the girl is very young and some die through blood loss. There are other serious complications. Sometimes healing is so tight that the flow of urine is impeded, and huge bladder stones are formed. A knife is used before intercourse is possible and the knife is used again to allow a baby to be born.

Valerie is now able to say to the women, 'Where in the Koran does it say that you must do this to your young girls?'

Those who can now read say, 'We have looked, and we cannot find it.'

Then Valerie says, 'If, as you believe, God has made you perfect, why are you interfering with His creation.' That is usually enough for them to rethink their old tradition. If not, Valerie's next step is to request a filming of FGM. When that is shown to the men, they are horrified and put pressure on the women to stop it. (FGM has always been secret women's business).

There are other harmful practices, particularly around childbirth. With the advent of literacy, Valerie has been able to train some of the bright women to be teachers in their own right. They have become powerful advocates for safe and effective practices.

We met Dr Enid Parker again on our return to Addis Ababa. We were able to tell her about the literacy classes. She was delighted to hear about the passion to learn. She and Margaret took us to lunch at one of the city's older hotels. The dining room was immaculate with perfect white starched table linen. Floral decoration was plentiful and tasteful. A white grand piano was being played skilfully by

Ethiopia's equivalent of Liberace. What a contrast that was to Logia and Assaita!

During the meal it was more evident than before that we were in the presence of a very dedicated and talented lady. Her vision had its origins in the Gospel. She epitomised what the Apostle Paul described in his letter to the Ephesians. 'For we are God's workmanship, created in Christ Jesus to do good works, which God prepared in advance for us to do.'[21] It was always Dr Enid's foremost desire that the Afar should know Jesus. Her translation of the New Testament into Afar must have been the pinnacle of her life's work.

Although the Afar are almost all Muslim, 60–70% of the highlanders are Christians. The Ethiopian Orthodox church is as old as the church in Rome. Although myths have crept into the orthodox belief, it is not difficult to find some fine Christians amongst the highlanders.

On another visit, I was invited to visit a leprosy hospital in Addis Ababa. There I was taken to the men's ward where a number had completed their treatment and were about to be discharged. One young man, who spoke quite good English beckoned me to his bedside. He handed me a letter imploring me to help him. He was destitute. He had no family to care for him and no job to go to. This was a typical story. The next man was in a similar situation. But instead of asking for help he showed me his Amharic Bible. He explained that he was sharing what he read with the other men in the ward. He was not just literate. He had found

---

[21] Ephesians 2: 10 – New international Version

solace in the eternal Word of God. And he was eager not to keep that Word to himself.

On yet another visit, Andrew took me to a service in a protestant church. Emblazoned in big, bold Amharic letters high on the front wall were the words of Jesus. In English, it reads, 'Come to me, all you that are weary and are carrying heavy burdens, and I will give you rest.'[22] This clear invitation of Jesus is there for all who hear or read these words. Jesus invites everyone regardless of their intellectual abilities. It is those who are literate who have the glorious responsibility of sharing the good news and encouraging others to hear and read.

---

[22] Matthew 11: 28 – New Revised Standard Version

Healing

On our third morning in Addis Ababa Andrew and I crossed the city to visit Dr Catherine Hamlin. Valerie escorted us all the way to the hospital. First we walked down her street. It is steep and had been cobbled to prevent erosion in the rainy season. We turned right opposite Footsum's house and immediately left down an unmade street which functions as a permanent marketplace. It was flanked on one side by a dusty soccer field. Progress was impeded by sheep and goats lying and standing. They would not move, so we had to walk around them. At the bottom of the street were donkeys submerged by huge loads of hay. We crossed the main road out of Val's suburb and headed for the next trunk route via a cross street which doubled as a bazaar. Plying a straight course was impossible. There were interruptions by vendors, beggars, animals and children. Cars and trucks were forced likewise to travel at a walking pace.

The bazaar led to the bus stop on the trunk road. Here a profusion of blue Toyota mini-buses plied their trade. Each one took 12 passengers, and each had a young boy who was the conductor. He would leap out at every stop and tout for business by announcing his bus's destination. The fares were cheap by Australian standards. A few cents would take one five or six kilometres. The big Fiat buses were cheaper still. But they were always packed tight and the risk of being pickpocketed or being exposed to a contagious disease such as TB was too great.

Our destination was the Swiss embassy. From there, we walked up a dirt street till we saw a sign advertising the Fistula Hospital. The grounds were guarded by a high wall and a stout iron gate. A very polite guard welcomed us, and we were escorted through the main hospital ward and into the operating theatre. There Dr Hamlin showed us the tiny change room and the cups of tea, which were most welcome.

The operating theatre accommodated three operating tables. The surgeons that day were Dr Hamlin; Dr Ambye, a skilled Ethiopian; Dr Howard, a Norwegian Lutheran missionary and Mamite, a former patient and also very skilled. Catherine came with her husband, Reg, to Addis Ababa in 1959. They founded their own hospital in 1974.[23] Mamite learnt her trade entirely at the Fistula Hospital. She has been observed by surgical specialists from London and could not be faulted.

One anaesthetist managed all three patients with spinal blocks. They were perfectly awake throughout the procedure, although they had no sensation below the waist. I was aware of three pairs of dark frightened eyes. The nurses would comfort the patients as best they could. The fistulae were mostly holes between the bladder and vagina and averaged 2.5 cms across. Sometimes there a hole between the rectum and vagina. The presence of a fistula

---

[23] The Hospital by the River – Dr Catherine Hamlin with John Little Pan Macmillan – 2001

meant constant uncontrollable leakage of urine and possibly bowel contents. The sufferer was invariably divorced by her husband and denied normal social interaction. Unsurprisingly some committed suicide. The basic cause of the fistula is the lack of medical assistance when there is an obstructed labour. That complication is easily rectified in Western countries by an assisted delivery, usually a Caesarean section. Fistula formation with childbirth does not therefore occur in the West.

After the operating list, Dr Hamlin showed us around the ward which accommodated 50 patients. After the fistula repair, the patients were rested for two weeks with a catheter in situ. A veranda outside the ward was reserved for Bible classes and various craft activities. One adjoining room was reserved for the projection of the "Jesus" film with the words in Amharic.

Patients lived with their fistula for years. The baby was usually stillborn after a labour lasting many days. Because of the continuous leakage of urine the poor woman would be totally ostracised. Her husband will have left her; she would have no social contact and would be housed in a hut on her own at the edge of her village.

Many, probably most, sufferers turn to begging as the only way to survive. They try to keep themselves dry by adopting a squatting position. When staying in that position for months and possibly years a fixed deformity occurs. The knees are stuck in flexion and the hips in adduction. It then takes months of physiotherapy to correct this before it is possible to repair the fistula.

There was always a joyful transformation when the fistula was repaired. There was not just physical healing, but mental, social and spiritual healing as well. It is no exaggeration to say that a fistula repair is life changing. On discharge from the hospital, each patient was given new clothes and a joyful send-off. They would be able to marry again and have a family. However they were warned that it was too risky to attempt a normal birth. Dr Hamlin's constant advice was, 'When you feel the baby walking around inside you start walking to a hospital.'[1] That would give them four months to reach the safety of medical assistance. Most subsequent babies would be born by Caesarean section to prevent the recurrence of a fistula.

Back in the Afar Ismael was determined to show us some of the medical needs of his society. From Assaita, he took us to Dupti, a town upstream and close to the Awash River. It boasted the only hospital serving about 2½ million Afar. The building looked quite new. At the entrance, we were welcomed by a most courteous white coated medical superintendent. He was an Amharic physician and spoke excellent English. We were first shown the operating theatre. In one corner was a new anaesthetic machine still in its plastic wrapping. The hospital had no surgeon and no supply of anaesthetic gases. Caesarean sections were the only operations performed. They were performed very rarely, and spinal blocks were employed.

We were shown the x-ray department and the pathology laboratory. Tests were limited to blood counts and bacterial cultures. When we saw the patients, it was evident that most were in hospital because of chronic illnesses such as TB and debilitating malaria. We were shown the plans of an ambitious building program to enlarge the hospital. We wondered where they would find the staff to run it.

Before we settled into our hotel accommodation, Ismael was determined to show us a geological curiosity. We crossed the Awash River via a narrow wooden bridge. In open country, Ismael gave orders to the driver as we meandered over sand dunes. There was much argument in Afar and no one seemed to know where we were going. Evidently Ismael was trying to find an area of boiling mud, but it remained elusive. There is an extensive area of volcanic activity in the Afar. To the North of Dupti are eight active volcanoes, some with the only permanent pools of molten lava in the world. Hot rock comes close to the surface in many areas and there is the constant risk of earthquakes. An Italian company explored the possibility of harnessing geothermal power. Ismael explained that it could have produced a copious supply of electricity. The Italians performed many successful drillings; but then abandoned the project because of political instability.

The search for boiling mud was not entirely wasted. One of the Afar elders travelling with us picked up something off the sand. He wrapped it in a handkerchief and proudly announced he had a cure for my arthritis (whether I had arthritis or not). It turned out he had some ostrich dung which he would make into an effective poultice!

Valerie explained to us that some of the Afar bush medicine was quite remarkable. For example, they had developed an herbal preparation which she felt sure accelerated the recovery from acute hepatitis A.

Back in Dupti we were invited to a coffee ceremony next door to our hotel. It was the home of a lady who had been a chanteuse in Djibouti and had fled the civil war. She looked very unwell, and we supposed she had chronic malaria and probably TB. She appeared to be very anaemic and had a productive cough. But with all that her hospitality was outstanding. I felt very humbled by her generosity.

Back at the hotel I came across another example of local friendliness. A young girl spotted me washing my clothes in half an old tractor tyre and offered to help. (The tractor tyre is the usual equipment for the purpose.) I rewarded the girl with several coins. She went away and returned with two fresh carrots and a broad smile.

That evening the streets of Dupti were extraordinarily festive. We were not told what they were celebrating. Perhaps Dupti is always a happy place! We turned in for a good night's rest as the next day would be a busy one.

The next morning we set off across the Awash River once again and joined a well-marked track. Our first stop was a run-down looking village. One of the buildings was a government clinic which was absolutely filthy. Its function was to provide vaccinations and first aid; but one would imagine that bugs would proliferate rather than be conquered. The villagers were employed on a nearby cotton plantation which was controlled by the Amhara.

Leaving the village we followed the banks of irrigation channels. Our Landcruiser got bogged a few times and unfortunately our driver, Daniel, had no previous experience in this sort of terrain. When we reached open country, there was the edge of a thorn bush forest to our left. This marked the limit of the river's flood plain. To our right there were bare rocky hills. We passed occasional herdsmen with camels. One camel was laden with his master's house, a deboita. This hemispherical dwelling is made of curved sticks and matting and is packed easily onto one camel.

Eventually we arrived at a complete mobile village. It consisted of several deboitas surrounded by corrals for the animals. Each corral was made of a circle of thorn bush branches. They are effective deterrents against would be escapees because the thorns are prolific, strong and 5 cms long. There were five corrals, one each for the cattle, sheep, goats, camels and baby camels. It was not explained why the baby camels had a corral to themselves while the young of the other animals were with the adults.

Upon our arrival, I was ushered into a deboita where a mother had just given birth to her seventh child. She was in a lot of pain, and I was expected to consult. There was minimal bleeding and the placenta (afterbirth) had been successfully delivered. Fortunately, the pain was explained by severe after pains which tend to be more pronounced with successive births. The new-born baby looked very well. But his future was not assured. Three of this woman's babies had died and the infant mortality in the region was a staggering 35%. And that does not include stillbirths and deaths within the first 28 days of life.

Having reassured the mother the serious business of celebrating the birth began. A bowl of fresh milk appeared. I was not told whether it was from a cow, a goat or a camel. For special occasions, it should be camels'. The bowl was passed around and it would have been in very poor taste to have refused a sip.

Margaret Monro, the Red Sea Missionary, gave me a nudge. As the elder present it fell to me to pronounce a blessing on the new-born baby. This was a huge privilege. I spoke in English asking for the blessing of Almighty God and Margaret translated into Afar. There were smiles all round.

We were very pleased to leave the deboita as the heat was very oppressive. Even though it was the cooler time of the year, the outside temperature would have been in the mid-30s. Inside there was a small fire burning, presumably for ritual cleansing. Also the deboita was crowded with two low couches, one occupied by the mother and the other providing seating for Valerie, Margaret, two older women, one highly pregnant young girl, myself and a goat!

During the following night I was introduced to some of the livestock. Valerie, Ismael and Aisha slept in a deboita. Daniel, the driver slept in the Landcruiser, and Andrew Margaret and I slept on mats in the open in the centre of the village. The mats were laid on thick dust and we each had a simple frame to support a mozzie net. A few men were stationed on the edge of the encampment on the side opposite the thorn bush forest. Their job, with the help of dogs was to ward off human and animal invaders. Hyenas were prowling around, and Issar cattle rustlers were a constant worry. The men were armed and would fire off into the darkness from time to time.

The nearest corral to my sleeping mat was for the goats. One wretched animal had a loud and persistent cough.

I had not noticed when we went to bed that there was one cow left in the centre of the village and outside the cattle corral. Just before midnight she came over to me and gave me a nudge. Like most African cows she had long horns. That did not worry me because I had been brought up with dairy cows. Having made her introduction she moved off into the shadows and about a half hour later I was aware of a persistent licking sound. Straining my eyes I could just make out her new-born calf. Then to my amazement she appeared to consume the afterbirth without it touching the deep dust on the ground. When the job was completed, she came over to me and gave me another nudge with her nose. Naturally, I congratulated her. The next morning I recounted the event. It seemed that I was the only one who was awake at that time; but the general opinion was that it was most appropriate that the cow should report to the obstetrician!

About three hours before dawn a loud scratching noise appeared to come from the nearest deboita. That was the sound of one of the ladies of the house grinding grain. The back breaking job was repeated every morning. Enough fresh flour had to be produced each day to feed the whole family. The lady made the flour into dough and lit a fire between rocks in the ground. She would then scrape out the coals and stick the dough onto the hot rock. The bread was consumed, and none was left till the next day because it would then be full of maggots. The grinding machines waiting on Valerie's veranda in Addis Ababa would make life easier for some of these hard-working women.

Life expectancy for women in that part of the world is less than for men and is less than 50 years. The women look after the sheep and goats as well as the household. They have the arduous task of fetching water, and this can mean a journey on foot of tens of kilometres each way. Whenever they have spare time they weave the mats to replace the ones which rapidly wear out on the roof and floor. The men seemed to have much less work to do. Beyond caring for the cattle and camels and carrying their weapons I could not identify any other responsibility.

When we returned to Addis Ababa, I was again made aware of the suffering in Valerie's household. I was summoned to see Subeeb who had abdominal pain. I suspected she was pregnant and could have an ectopic pregnancy. A pregnancy test was positive, and the pain rapidly settled. Some months later I heard that she was safely delivered of a healthy baby.

Big Aisha had debilitating filariasis. This is a parasitic disease and can proceed to elephantiasis. Doctors Luke and Phillippe from MSF (Medecins sans Frontieres) very kindly called to review the patient. These men were from France and Belgium respectively and presented themselves as very caring physicians. Abdulla, the young man with the claw hands and amputated right leg, never ceased to amaze me. Each morning I was fascinated to see how skilfully he strapped on his artificial leg.

Valerie's household was a microcosm of suffering and the need for healing. Those burdened young people were representatives of Afar society. Abdulla reminded me of the persecution those people have suffered at the hands of the Issar, a stronger and more numerous group. I was reminded of the injuries that so many young men had suffered in trying to defend their land. I was reminded too of those who had lost their lives and those who had fled And become refugees because of real threats to their lives.

Big Aisha was a reminder of the massive health problems of the Afar. Recurring droughts with resulting malnutrition take a huge toll on the wellbeing of so many Afar. I was reminded of the very sick people I had met. There were those with severe anaemia from chronic malaria and those with long standing TB.

The people I met needed healing from so many problems. I felt helpless. I had no magic bullets. But I could give them some hope.

Valerie and Ismael had founded their own indigenous organisation to help the Afar people who received little help from the Ethiopian federal government. It is the Afar Pastoral Development Association. It is funded by international gifts from various sources. It was in its infancy when I visited in 1996. But I could help to fund their activities.

Valerie set about training nurses and midwives. Funding them would bring hope for the healing of many diseases. Vaccination programs would prevent many more. 15 years later she opened a hospital funded by the Barbara May Foundation Australia.[24] This focuses on women's health and is the only hospital of its kind in the Afar region.

The health of the animals was paramount because the people's wealth lay with their livestock. And so a veterinary program has brought healing for the animals.

Ismael promoted engineering works. Roads have been built to gain ambulance access to the more remote areas. Most importantly water catchment devices have been built to harvest storm water.

As the time for my departure drew near I searched for something meaningful to leave with Valerie's household. I have recorded the hope expressed for a better temporal future. I was left with the thought of sharing the spiritual hope I have. Valerie was most agreeable that I should read a passage from the Apostle Paul's second letter to the

---

[24] www.barbaramayfoundation.com

Corinthians, chapter five. I read about Jesus' ministry of reconciliation, of how the relationship with God could be healed and how important that was. I ended at chapter six, verse two, "Now is the time of salvation".

Ismael read the whole passage in Afar. Then to my amazement Abdulla got up and spoke energetically to the whole group. Although he spoke in Afar, I understood that he was encouraged by what we had read. Later that evening I gave him my battered Aussie hat. He was visibly touched by that simple gesture.

As I entered Ethiopia at the beginning of that memorable visit I had just finished reading the biography of Bishop Festo Kivengere. He was a great African and one of the most gifted evangelists of the twentieth century. Bishop Festo noted that no one was ever converted by theological argument. They responded to a vision of Christ's love.[25] Christ's love has certainly been visible in the ministries of both Dr Catherine Hamlin and Valerie. They have been powerful agents for healing, both physical and spiritual.

---

[25] Missionary Reconciliation: The Role of the Doctrine of Reconciliation in the Preaching of Bishop Festo Kivengere of Uganda 1971–1988 – Alfred Olwa.

Annus Horribilis

For me, 1999 was an "annus horribilis", horrible year. It began with a near death on the operating table. We were delivering a baby by a routine Caesarean section. The mother asked for an epidural block. I inserted it (I had many years of experience with epidurals) but when it promised not to give adequate pain relief the anaesthetist took over. She commenced a general anaesthetic. When she had administered, the intravenous drugs and had inserted a tube into the trachea to maintain the airway there was sudden collapse. The pulse was weak and there was patchy cyanosis. The anaesthetist assumed the endotracheal tube was not properly placed, removed it and reinserted it. There was no improvement in the patient's condition. Clearly the lives of both mother and baby were at risk. The mother's circulation was seriously impaired. The cause was not apparent. They were very tense moments. Every second counted. Except for the anaesthetist no one dared speak.

The anaesthetist was panicking, and it was difficult for the rest of us to remain calm. Calm was needed for clear thinking and appropriate action. I cursed the fact that I was called up in the wee small hours of the previous night. I had attended a confinement and consequently my "thinking cap" was not fully charged. All of us in the theatre felt helpless.

A consultant physician was called, and he advised the administration of adrenaline. To our great relief there was an immediate response. I rapidly delivered the baby by Caesarean section. His circulation was also compromised; but happily both mother and baby responded to resuscitation, and both were well thereafter.

To witness the near death of a healthy young mother was a shocking experience. It certainly exhausted me. Although there is teamwork in the operating theatre, the surgeon must take ultimate responsibility for the patient's safety. After the operation, the nurses met for de-briefing and counselling. I was barred from that meeting, a fact which I found very disturbing. The anaesthetist sought succour from her colleagues as she was a staff specialist and had the assistance of an association of salaried doctors. Being a visiting medical officer I enjoyed no such support. There was in fact not a single colleague I could turn to.

The hospital administration set up a formal investigation and a senior anaesthetist from a teaching hospital in Sydney was engaged to conduct an enquiry. He proposed that the cause of the patient's collapse was the introduction of air into her circulation when the uterus (womb) was opened, exposing uterine veins to the outside. He further postulated that this was made more likely following the abandonment of the epidural block. As I was the one who had attempted the epidural block I must take responsibility for the patient's collapse. This seemed to me a most unlikely scenario as the patient collapsed before I opened the uterus and performed the Caesarean section. Furthermore the membranes holding the water around the baby were still intact. There was therefore no possible access to uterine veins from the external air when the collapse occurred. My own conclusion was that the visiting consultant's hypothesis was wrong; but apart from the consultant physician no one agreed with me.

Later, when the patient was well enough to undertake some comprehensive testing, it transpired that the actual cause of her collapse was an anaphylactic reaction to suxamethonium. This is a drug used in the induction of a general anaesthetic. Its purpose is to temporarily paralyse the muscles to allow the easy introduction of the endotracheal tube and the efficient artificial oxygenation of the patient. Anaphylaxis is the name given to a very severe allergic reaction when, as we witnessed, there is circulatory collapse. Many chemicals can be responsible for anaphylaxis and its fatal consequences are well known. Some of the most widely known causes are food items, particularly some nuts.

About this time my colleague and specialist partner suddenly resigned. That immediately increased my workload. Instead of being on a manageable one in two roster I immediately found myself on call continuously. (I understand that today the specialists are accepting nothing more onerous than a one in three roster). My requests for relief directed to the hospital administration and to senior staff in Sydney fell on deaf ears. It felt as if I was being punished, as if my colleague's resignation was my fault. I was concerned that, with the inevitable lack of sleep, my clinical judgment would soon show signs of failing. From previous experience, I knew that sleepless nights could have a very dangerous effect. My desire was always that the safety of my patients should not be compromised.

Also about this time an acute medical problem had to be managed at home. Pressures at home and pressures at work drained any energy I had left. Would there be an end to it? Would anyone answer my call for help? My faith was being sorely tested. I had always relied on the goodness of God. He had upheld me during and after my near-death experience on the road in 1978. But this time it seemed as if He was abandoning me. I was losing all hope. This combination of awful events was proving too much to bear. It was for me much more difficult to handle than the aftermath of the car accident. A familiar verse from the psalms came to mind, "My God, my God, why have you forsaken me?" Hope for relief was dwindling rapidly. When it was all over, I had to confess that although my faith almost failed completely He remained faithful.

A locum was eventually provided. It turned out that he was inexperienced, and I was tempted to think he was sent from the larger hospital to a unit where it was assumed he required less knowledge. Of course the reverse is true. In a smaller hospital, one must be prepared to face every possible emergency on one's own. It is just not good enough to assume that all the serious problems will be dealt with in the big hospitals. Needless to say this locum did not stay very long.

The time came to speak frankly with the hospital administration. It would have been better to talk to a colleague who also had an administrative role. Most hospitals have medical superintendents. They are medically qualified and therefore should be empathetic to the concerns of individual doctors. In the largest hospitals, the role of the medical superintendent is usually filled by someone who is very knowledgeable and understanding of other doctors' problems. But in smaller hospitals the medical superintendent would be a part time job. It would more likely to be a person who had not made a success in medical practice and had fallen into a clerical role by default. In that case, he or she will be under the thumb of the general manager.

The general managers are usually people with no direct medical experience and their primary responsibility is to see that the hospital operates within its budget. He or she is governed by regulations set up by bureaucrats, who also have no medical experience. In an ideal situation, there should be a robust system of clinical governance. This is where decisions about workplace performance and the investigation of unsatisfactory outcomes are managed by peers. That means that doctors manage doctors, nurses manage nurses and so on.

I was privileged, more than ten years previously, to help establish systems of peer review, quality assurance and delineation of clinical privileges in the same rural hospital. It was only partly successful because there was never a wholehearted commitment by peers to oversee the system. But the theory was good, and we should have worked harder to make it work.

As it was, peer review, quality assurance and delineation of clinical privileges were taken over largely by bureaucrats who were not medically trained. And there was no one other than the general manager for me to address my concerns.

In this instance, the general manager was defensive. There were more senior people to answer to in Sydney. My complaints were met seemingly without an ounce of sympathy. Why did I have to shoulder the blame for the near death in the operating theatre when the cause was a totally unanticipated reaction to an anaesthetic drug? Apparently the record could not be changed. Why was there next to no help in providing a suitable locum? No explanation was forthcoming.

Eventually there was good news. The hospital had advertised for not one, but two permanent replacements for my colleague who resigned. And two keen, skilled and energetic gentlemen arrived about nine months after the commencement of my annus horribilis. I could at last relax. Faith was restored. Praise God! The following year was a year of celebration. Early in that year the Rector of our church graciously asked me to share my experiences with the whole congregation. Many found It helpful to listen to the story of my trials and tribulations. They understood my account of losing hope and of wondering if God cared. Being able to share that was a powerful exercise in restoring my faith.

Mercifully, there were no serious outcomes during my awful year apart for the near death on the operating table. The experience emphasised the importance and need of genuine teamwork.

After I retired, I was privileged to take part in what our college called Practice Visitation. This was a bold step and was introduced as a major option in compulsory continuing medical education. Two peers, senior specialists in Obstetrics and Gynaecology, examined a colleague's practice. Prior to a visit we surveyed a large batch of patients' records. The visit itself lasted two full days. The two of us interviewed everyone who impacted with the specialist practice apart from the patients themselves. We therefore met other doctors such as the anaesthetist and the paediatrician. We interviewed the senior nursing staff in the labour ward, the main wards and the operating theatre. We also spoke to the clerical staff and surgery receptionist. We observed the specialist in the operating theatre.

We sent a report to the Royal Australian and New Zealand College of Obstetricians and Gynaecologists (RANZCOG). This was edited and sent back to the specialist who had just been visited. The whole exercise was deemed to be just as valuable for those who made the visit as it was for those being visited. Later I was asked to give an appraisal of the Practice Visitations program to the presidents of the other medical colleges. The RANZCOG had been in the forefront of continuing medical education and the other colleges had nothing like this in place. That meeting was held at Sydney Airport making it easier for participants coming from interstate. The response to my talk was disappointing. Perhaps I was not persuasive enough? I hoped I sounded enthusiastic as I certainly found the experience of the visits very encouraging. As it happened the specialists in our own college who took part were almost exclusively from rural and regional parts of Australia. Apparently the city members saw no need for this exercise. It seemed the other college presidents were of the same mind.

Another survey I was involved in was a perinatal review. This was undertaken by a two-person team, one obstetrician and one paediatrician. The idea was to gather data and interview all those responsible for the safe and effective supervision of childbirth and the care of new-born babies in a particular hospital. I visited hospitals in Dubbo and Albany. Again I found it an encouraging exercise. Again it was done on a peer-to-peer basis. Both exercises were non-threatening and during the whole process a sense of camaraderie was palpable.

My own experience of my "annus horribilis" and subsequent experiences of peer review led me to wonder what was lacking in many hospitals. If good teamwork is to be a reality, ergo, there must be good relationships between individual staff at all levels. Sadly, that is not always present, and the reverse sometimes rears an ugly head. According to the national news the lack of good teamwork has taken on a more odious aspect in some hospitals. Reports have been published of bullying in at least three teaching hospitals in Sydney. Senior doctors, generally surgeons have been responsible for serious verbal abuse of junior doctors.

What then is necessary to introduce and maintain good relationships? There is no better starting point than to look at the example and words of Jesus. Just before his crucifixion Jesus' central command to His disciples was this. 'I give you a new commandment, that you love one another. Just **as I have loved you,** you also should love one another.'[26] This is the basis of all wholesome relationships, including, of course, professional teams. St Paul wrote 'Let love be genuine.' [27]What he wrote and what Jesus said was about the kind of love which puts others' needs before self-interest. Jesus was and is our supreme example. Before His arrest, trial and crucifixion, He demonstrated the humility of a

---

[26] John 13: 34 – NRSV
[27] Romans 12: 9 – NRSV

perfect leader. He washed His disciples' feet. That showed that He expected them also, as leaders, "to get their hands dirty" in the service of their mates. The love Jesus demonstrated was powerful and sacrificial.

So how does this love express itself in the professional setting? How, in practice should we put the interests of others before our own?

The first prerequisite for a good relationship with others is to be a good listener. This might sound trite; but it is clear that problems in all working relationships start when one person fails to listen properly to a colleague. This is particularly important when administrators employ a carefully prescribed format to investigate an incident without giving enough time to each person involved in the incident. When a senior colleague or administrator is listening to a complaint from a junior, it must be very tempting to butt in. The official policy has to be heard. But the official policy must wait for the complaint to be stated in detail, especially if the complaint is one of bullying. It may well be better at the first meeting for the senior colleague or administrator to say nothing of substance, but simply to listen.

Some years ago a survey in general medical practice concluded that it was best not to interrupt a patient's story. No matter how verbose the patient may be the doctor was found to deliver better treatment if he listened carefully to every word the patient uttered. He could ask questions to explore the patient's complaint in greater depth; but that should wait till the patient finished their initial narrative.

In the same way when investigating a complaint brought by a junior member of staff, it is vital that the complainant be given full rein. That person must be allowed the respect that is due to everyone who comes looking for support in a particular issue.

There are several parts to good listening. Obviously, one is taking in every detail. There must be an attitude of concentration. One's body language and eye contact demonstrate that one is genuinely interested and genuinely listening. One must convey the impression that one is working towards a satisfactory conclusion.

One important outcome of good listening is affirmation. When one listens to any story, it will become clear that the person giving that story has made points that are worthy of praise. Those points must be acknowledged. Praise must be given whenever it is due. In the case of bullying, the complainant may have put up with verbal abuse for a significant length of time. If that is the case, it must be recognised, and the complainant complimented for bearing with it for so long.

If a senior colleague or administrator is reprimanding a junior during the course of investigating a particular poor patient outcome, it is vital to find something positive first. No one is so bad at the job that there is nothing good that that can be said. If that were the case, that person would not have been employed in the first place. No, there is always a point of affirmation to be found first. It is not just a kindness to make that point; but it also establishes a good relationship. By first affirming, the good one can address the problem of the poor outcome in an atmosphere of good will and understanding.

When a marriage is on the rocks, it is good if the counsellor can start with affirmation. Experience bears out that if each partner can verbalise something good about the other, even if it is something trivial, that is a fruitful way to begin. It puts the partners at ease and assists the process of initiating reconciliation.

Jesus' command to love one another means that every relationship must be characterised by real caring. I was privileged many times to address the recruits at the NSW police academy. That was in my role as a member of Gideons International. In the early days, each recruit was required to accept a pocket Testament (New Testament, Psalms and Proverbs) on which the oath of allegiance to Queen and Commonwealth was sworn at the passing out parade. Later that stipulation was relaxed, and the recruits could use the holy book of their choosing or simply swear an affirmation. We were given ½ hour to speak to them before offering the gift of the Testament.

I had had personal contact with an officer who subsequently committed suicide. He was in the federal police and worked under cover. The personal pressures imposed on such duties would be much higher than with general duties. Nevertheless I felt there was an opportunity to tell the assembled recruits about the importance of caring for one another, to look after each member of the team. No one had noticed that the man who died was depressed before he took his life.

The senior person in every professional organisation has a special duty to care for the junior staff. That should be in the terms of employment. But sadly we are informed that the captains of industry, the managers and directors of companies as well as senior government appointees are too often self-serving. Financial success is too often seen as more important than a harmonious working environment.

Throughout the health industry there are pressures and stresses which do not exist in other industries. Medical and surgical care has to be provided right around the clock. Emergencies have to be attended to immediately. That can be at any hour of the day and night. Therefore it is incumbent on all senior staff to care for the emotional and spiritual wellbeing of all members of their teams.

Genuine harmony in a team demands trusting relationships. There are several more facets to this. Honesty, humility and a willingness to admit mistakes are among them. There is also the need to spend time mentoring other members of the team. This includes providing an opportunity for early de-briefing whenever an unsatisfactory outcome occurs.

If one is in any doubt about what is required for harmonious relationships, one need look no further than to the words and example of Jesus.

International Peace

During the period of the Cold War doctors were very much aware of the potential for nuclear annihilation. We had all seen the pictures of the devastation wrought by atom bombs on Hiroshima and Nagasaki. We were all aware of the horrific consequences of exposure to radiation. After WWII, there was a frantic arms race. The combined nuclear arsenals of the USA, Russia, Britain and France could wipe out the whole human race many times over. It later became very concerning that other nations developed their own nuclear military capabilities. These included China, India, Pakistan, N Korea and Israel.

In 1974, I joined the international organisation, Doctors against Nuclear War. There were and are likeminded physicians all around the world including many behind the "Iron Curtain". Because the Cold War was still very much in evidence it was agreed that there should be conversations between East and West. Doctors in the West were "twinned" with doctors in the communist bloc. I was partnered with another gynaecologist and obstetrician in Hungary. He and I began regular correspondence. We immediately understood that we both held the same objectives and ideals. We were both adamant that world-wide nuclear disarmament was and still is a top priority.

There were opportunities to share our concerns in the medical and national presses. I was once privileged to be a signatory to a letter going to both presidents of the United States and Russia urging them to negotiate for nuclear arms reduction.

After the fall of the "Iron Curtain" in 1989, it became more attractive to travel to Eastern Europe. After my *annus horribilis* in 1999, there was an opportunity to take an overseas holiday. Two new specialists had been appointed and that afforded very adequate cover for the work at the hospital. My wife and I made plans to visit her family in England and my colleague in Hungary. And so for us the year 2000 was a year of exploration and excitement.

Our hosts, my colleague and his wife, Feri and Margit, met us at Budapest airport. There they presented us with a bouquet of flowers and took us to our hotel. That may sound a little strange as we were their guests. But their government had decreed that all tourists must stay in a hotel for the first one or two nights. That would naturally boost their tourist industry. Our hosts were most gracious and understood the government's rule.

Our hotel overlooked the Danube, and we had a wonderful view during dinner. It was May and we enjoyed a bright evening. The famous Chain Bridge was clearly seen to our right. Opened in 1849 it was designed by an Englishman and built by a Scottish engineer and at the time was the only bridge across the Danube in Budapest.

The next day Feri and Margit took us to see St Stephen's Basilica. This cathedral was built in honour of Stephen, the first Christian king of Hungary, 975–1038 AD. We thought we were alone in that grand building until we noted an elderly couple with a priest in the sanctuary. The magnificent baroque organ began to play. Our host explained that the couple was celebrating their diamond wedding anniversary and renewing their vows. We shared thoughts of how wonderful it must have been for them.

My doctor colleague and his wife then took us to their home in Székesfehérvár. They live in a flat on the third floor of a large amorphous concrete block built in the communist era. Theirs is a most humble abode, as no doubt are all the others. Their two children, now grown up and left home, were brought up in that cramped home. While the communists were in power, the doctors were awarded a paltry salary. When the Russians left, there was an opportunity to commence private practice. Some doctors became wealthy by "double dipping". They were paid by the government and collected private fees from the same patients. My colleague would not enter into any unethical practice and remained poor. He was however greatly admired for his knowledge and skill.

The flat consisted of a lounge room, dining room, bedroom, kitchen, bathroom and toilet. Every room was very small. The dining room was furnished with a narrow table and chairs. The backs of the chairs on each side were against the walls. The kitchen was tiny. The toilet and bathroom were both so cramped that we had to walk in sideways! Our hosts insisted we use their bed while they slept in the lounge room. The double bed occupied most of the room. It came apart in the middle so that the lower half could be pushed under the upper half to allow more room during the day.

Margit is an excellent cook. Her nickname is "Mrs Lipton" because she is fond of tea. We felt that we were treated royally with such generous hospitality. The couple kept their flat in immaculate condition and viewed from the street it was clear that theirs was the most attractive. It was the only one adorned with window boxes. And being springtime the colours were magnificent.

Feri entertained us wonderfully. 2000 was the 250th anniversary of the death of J S Bach (1685–1750) and to mark the occasion a sextet from Nice had come to perform in the cathedral in Székesfehérvár. The four of us enjoyed a wonderful concert. The setting added to the atmosphere and the building enhanced the sound of Bach's music. Nearby was the bishop's palace. My colleague accepted that because of the foregoing history it was appropriate for such a senior RC prelate to be accommodated sumptuously. But he was very critical of a local protestant pastor whose modern home was certainly much more sumptuous than his. If he wanted to attract the local population, he felt that pastor should live more humbly!

Outside of Székesfehérvár is the excavated Roman town of Gorsium. A visit to this carefully exposed monument is a tourist "must". The 'Hungarian Riviera' is also a great attraction. Hungary is land-locked; but the country is blessed with the largest freshwater lake in Central Europe. Lake Balaton has a shoreline of 197 kms. There are beaches and opportunities for sailing and other water sports. The surrounding hills are dotted with vineyards and the scenery is stunning.

Back in Székesfehérvár my friend was keen to show us a memorial to the great Ignaz Semmelweis – 1818–1865. He was born in Hungary and studied in Székesfehérvár before moving to Vienna. There in the maternity hospital he famously solved the problem of the high maternal mortality. Many women were dying of post-natal infection. Semmelweis discovered that they were being infected by attendants not washing their hands after working in the mortuary. Once simple antiseptic precautions were introduced the death rate plummeted.

Semmelweis is credited with other advances too and is honoured by having a university named after him in Budapest.

Feri took us on another tour of Budapest. In Buda, an ancient castle and other historic buildings bear the scars of war. Evidence of the German bombardment in this area in WW II has been preserved as a reminder of the devastation of war.

Before we left, my friend's son gave us a small book of Hungarian poetry. It is written by a Jew, Miklos Radnoti, who was imprisoned and finally executed by the Germans in WWII. He describes his experiences and tries to make sense of what he sees around him. In one poem, which especially appeals to me, he finds help as he reflects on the words of the prophet Isaiah. He converted to Christianity; but that did not save him from being executed by the Nazis just before the end of the war.

Our meeting with Feri and Margit and our introduction to the country of Hungary stimulated much thoughtfulness. Although the threat of nuclear war has never been matched in the past, Hungary has experienced many conflicts. Because of its position in central Europe there have been invasions by many warring tribes. It has been described by

Wikipedia as a crossroads for Celts, Romans, Germanic tribes, Huns, West Slavs and the Avars. As we noted the Romans occupied part of modern Hungary. Their province of Pannonia did not, however, extend northwards and eastwards beyond the Danube, so it only included the southwest section of the modern country. Then in the sixth century AD the Avars invaded. They came from central Asia and included the Mongols. It is their influence which gave the Hungarian language its uniqueness. Prince Arpad is accredited as being the founder of Hungary. He united the remaining invaders and older inhabitants. His great grandson, Stephen I, came to the throne in 1,000 AD. He converted the realm to a Christian kingdom. Hungary was invaded and partly occupied by the Ottoman Empire from 1541 to 1699. Thence the Hapsburgs ruled the country, and it became the eastern partner of the Austro-Hungarian Empire which was a major power in Europe till early in the twentieth century. Hungary suffered huge losses after WWI with the disappearance of 71% of its territory. 58% of the total population and 32% of ethnic Hungarians were no longer citizens of the new Hungary.

Modern Hungary has a population of nearly 10 million. There has been a significant Romani population. They, with the Jews and homosexuals, were targets for Nazi extermination in WWII. After WWII, the Soviet Union took Hungary as one of its satellites. Like other Eastern Bloc countries the people suffered privations under the communists. The fall of the Soviet Union in 1989 resulted in Hungary becoming a democratic republic. They joined the European Union in 2004 and also joined NATO.

Wars have been a major feature throughout the centuries. Empires have come and empires have gone. Wars and rumours of wars continue.

As I write this Vladimir Putin has invaded Ukraine, which is a near neighbour of Hungary's. The civil war in Ethiopia continues unabated. Jihadists hold sway in Mali. The brutal military regime in Myanmar continues to oppress its citizens. Life remains chaotic in Syria and Afghanistan. There are many other trouble spots around the world. I have not heard the latest figure, but only a few years ago the UN announced that there were no less than 40 conflicts waging around the world.

The need, the earnest desire, of the common people is for peace and prosperity. Genuine and lasting peace is the first priority. This is especially true for the people of Hungary. It has been an enormous privilege to have been a friend of Feri's for almost 50 years. International friendships are vital if genuine peace will prevail.

Jesus said, 'Blessed are the peacemakers, for they will be called the children of God.'[28] Those who follow Christ are those whose role it is to be His ambassadors, His agents. He, through the Holy Spirit, commits them to the role of promoting peace with God and thence peace amongst men. What a privilege! And what a daunting task! Can individuals really have any influence? Can they really make a difference?

When each and every individual truly follows Christ, he or she spreads the aroma of Christ. It was Christ, the Prince of Peace, who gave Himself up to death that those who

---

[28] Matthew 5: 9

believe in Him would have peace with God. That is the powerful message Christ's followers proclaim.

The Apostle Paul begins all his letters with the salutation "Grace to you and Peace". It is the grace of our Lord Jesus Christ working in us which gives us peace.

It is a blessed fact that there are Christian peacemakers in every nation on earth. Each person who is called by God becomes a child of God and a peacemaker in his or her local community. Each individual has limited influence. But the whole Body of Christ, that is the sum of all believers world-wide, can with God's help have tremendous influence. All of Christ's ambassadors, having the same urgent message, can, we pray, bring God's peace to a broken and divided world.

Justice and Mercy

In 1962, an exciting historical find was made at Guy's Hospital, London. In the dusty recesses of the medical school basement, a stash of Guy's Hospital Reports was uncovered. Dated 1839 and 1840 they contained clinical articles, some by such luminaries as Thomas Addison, Richard Bright and Sir Astley Cooper. The first two have well known diseases named after them and Sir Astley has given his name to several anatomical features. Each volume was priced at six shillings, a princely sum in 1840. The articles were illustrated with exquisite lithographs and each volume was fully bound, adding to the cost. They were sold in 1962 to any interested buyer for two shillings and sixpence each. Naturally, medical students in particular could not resist a bargain and I purchased two, one each of the April and October 1840 editions. I have since donated them to the medical history museum at Melbourne University.

In October 1840, the Guy's Hospital Reports advertised a course in "Medical Jurisprudence". This cost each student three guineas and one must assume it was money well spent. But the bachelor's degrees in medicine and surgery in the early 1960s did not contain a hint of teaching on the legal aspects of medical practice. Were we so blasé then? Did we feel the law would never impinge on our work? We were in for a shock. Both Britain and Australia followed the American trend and by the 1980s we were immersed in a sea of litigation. Sydney was to gain the reputation of being the second most litigious city in the world after Los Angeles.

But not all medico-legal matters involved litigation. My own experience was varied and soon after qualifying it was clear that occasional visits to courts of law were part of my duty in serving my patients.

My first appearance in court was at the request of the coroner. A lady in her thirties was involved in a car accident. She was eight months pregnant. Although she had abdominal pain, she was stable on arrival at our casualty department. The baby appeared to be none the worse for her mother's experience. Some upper abdominal tenderness did not indicate anything too serious at first. A chest X-ray did not reveal any mischief. Some hours later she collapsed and could not be revived. We were shocked. To our horror a post-mortem examination revealed ruptures in the liver, spleen and diaphragm. The uterus was intact and was in fact completely devoid of any sign of injury. The baby was therefore well protected; but unhappily it did not survive when the mother's heart stopped.

My appearance in the witness box was very brief. As the house surgeon on call in the casualty department I would have been the first doctor in the hospital to see the patient. But being very junior, only a few months out of medical school, it was left to more senior members of the surgical team to face most of the coroner's questioning.

The death of a mother eight months pregnant was a most tragic circumstance. It is a rare event in any hospital in the UK or Australia. When it does occur, it generates huge soul searching and is, arguably, more distressing than in any other category of patient death. It is worth noting that injury, such as from a road accident is one of the major causes of maternal death in the Western world. The maternal death rate is now at an almost irreducible low level. (This is not the case in the third world). But we did learn from that case. One of the injuries, which remained undiagnosed until the post-mortem, was the ruptured diaphragm. This injury alone was enough to be fatal as a subsequent case was to prove. But a plain X-ray taken with the patient standing or at least sitting up did not reveal it. A side-on X-ray with the patient lying down, a decubitus lateral, would have shown abdominal organs protruding into the chest. This would kill the patient by displacing the heart, as happened eight years later in another hospital.

A young lady, who was 20 weeks pregnant, was admitted to hospital with an acute attack of diarrhoea and vomiting. She was treated with intravenous fluids. Two days after admission, which happened to be a Sunday, she vomited copiously and collapsed. Efforts at resuscitation failed and she was pronounced dead. The experience was a dreadful shock to all the staff working that day. It was made worse by it being on a Sunday and consequently other more senior staff members were not so readily available.

A couple of days later the whole obstetric team, two consultants, two registrars in specialist training and two senior house officers, trooped into the mortuary where the pathologist, scalpel in hand, was about to conduct an autopsy. Before he made his long incision, he asked the assembled company what might be the cause of death. Before the heart stopped, cyanosis had developed. So someone suggested aspiration of vomit; but the collapse was too dramatic. We were all asking ourselves whether something could have been done to save the young lady's life. What could possibly explain such a catastrophe?

At that time, I was one of the two registrars. Thinking back to the road accident case I postulated that the young patient had a large undetected diaphragmatic hernia. This is a rare condition which is usually fatal or corrected surgically soon after birth. But what if a hernia had remained undetected for over 20 years?

The pathologist made his long incision, opening both the abdomen and the chest. To every one's surprise there was indeed a large defect in the diaphragm. It was on the left side. About three quarters of the bowel together with parts of the stomach, liver and spleen had been forced into the chest. This had compressed the lungs and explained the cyanosis. The coup de grace came as the heart was displaced violently to the right, cutting off the blood flow to the heart.

Could anything have been done to save this young life? First one would have to make a diagnosis and that could have been done with chest x-rays; but one would have to be very quick. Then one would have to relieve the pressure on the heart and lungs. That would need to be done very quickly. There would be no time to transfer the patient to the operating theatre. So incising the left side of the chest with a penknife or whatever was readily available in the ward would be the answer. And that would need huge courage and a firm belief in the diagnosis. Obviously, the chances of arriving at the correct diagnosis and saving this young life were remote in the extreme.

One mantra which was included in our clinical teaching was, 'Always expect the unexpected.' That sounds like a contradiction. But in the course of 30 or 40 years of a busy practice I inevitably came across some rare and unexpected complications. And that is one reason why it is vital to have a close-knit team of experienced consultants and junior doctors. The accumulated wisdom of all the members of a team is more likely to arrive at the correct diagnosis and then appropriate treatment can be given.

A third maternal death was in theory more preventable. A lady aged 36 was expecting her first baby. At that age, she was classified as an elderly primigravida. She had high blood pressure for several years and was under the supervision of a consultant physician. However her blood pressure was not well controlled during the pregnancy and the choice of blood pressure medication was limited. Towards the end of her pregnancy she was observed in hospital. On a Sunday (again), she showed protein in her urine for the very first time. This was an ominous sign. The consultant advised we induce labour the next day, Monday. Events turned rapidly for the worst. At about 2.00 a.m., that night I was called to her bedside. She had developed severe back pain which was situated in the ribcage just left of the spine. My physician colleague diagnosed a posterior myocardial infarct, a heart attack. There was nothing that could be done for her at that stage beyond making her more comfortable.

The patient's condition deteriorated very rapidly about breakfast time. She had the first of a series of grand mal convulsions, developed acute liver failure, had a cerebral haemorrhage and died. This all happened in the space of an hour or so. This was an example of eclampsia in its severest and most alarming form. Incidentally, eclampsia is the third most common cause of maternal death in the third world, after haemorrhage and infection. In the Western world, death from eclampsia is extremely rare, being prevented by diagnosis in its preliminary stages and the giving of appropriate treatment.

"Eclampsia" is derived from the Greek word for lightning and is so described because of the suddenness and drama of its appearance. However there are warning signs if one looks for them. The first is a rise in blood pressure; but in this case it was not a sign that we could use because the patient had pre-existing high blood pressure. There are blood tests which are helpful, but they were not in common use when this patient was being cared for. However, there was much soul searching following this death and we felt there must have been some sign that would have given us early warning of the impending doom.

To my recollection there was not a whiff of complaint from the next of kin of the three deceased ladies. There were, in theory, things that could have been done that might have saved their lives. And yet the families of all three deceased mothers were accepting of the circumstances of the deaths and never questioned the outcomes. That was all about to change. A veritable flood of litigation was soon to be unleashed. It was led by the Americans.

In 1969 and 1970, we observed several instances of unexpected rises in blood pressure following the injection of ergometrine. There was one instance of cardiac arrest. This happened under anaesthesia and followed immediately after giving ergometrine to help the uterus contract in the treatment of an incomplete miscarriage. Fortunately, the anaesthetist was monitoring the patient closely and started the heart again very promptly.

Ergometrine is an ergot alkaloid derived from rust, the fungus growing on rye. It causes the uterine muscle to contract strongly and was first used in the 1930s. It was most successful in limiting uterine bleeding and thereby saved many lives that would have been lost from post-partum haemorrhage. Its effect on the smooth muscle of the arterioles is unpredictable, hence the occasional surprise incidents of high blood pressure. These rises in blood pressure can be dangerously high.

My mentors, the obstetric consultants, encouraged me to publish the observations we had made. At that time, ergometrine was usually given routinely in combination with oxytocin as an intramuscular injection just after the baby was born. It went under the trade name of Syntometrine. It reduced blood loss and hastened the delivery of the placenta. Our recommendation was to abandon the routine use of ergometrine and to use oxytocin by itself. Many colleagues resisted the change; but as the years went by the use of oxytocin by itself proved to be perfectly adequate.

The medical article stimulated world-wide interest and requests for copies were legion, the larger number coming from Eastern Europe which was then behind the iron curtain. At the same time, a request came from the USA for me to appear as an expert witness in a case of medical litigation. They had evidently experienced a fatal outcome following the use of ergometrine. My reaction was to advise that they call a local expert. Not only were there ample senior and very knowledgeable practitioners in the USA; but also it is always more appropriate for experts who are familiar with the local medical scene to give evidence. This principal was not followed in a case against me, as we shall see.

The first case against me was heralded by a most abusive phone call. A couple who had adopted a baby phoned to say I had sold them a lemon! After a tirade of expletives they concluded the conversation by saying they would sue me for every cent I possessed.

The baby in question was born to a teenage mother who was given the nick name "wide eyes, wide thighs" by her GP. I recall she possessed a certain naivety! I first met her well into her pregnancy and it was evident to me that we were dealing with a smallish baby. I therefore did not let her go overdue, assuming the placenta to be less than perfectly healthy. The baby was well at birth and remained so for the next four weeks when I recorded an examination for adoption.

The baby subsequently displayed features of cerebral palsy. The abusive phone call was followed by a substantial claim alleging that I was remiss in not forecasting the disability. Unfortunately at that time there was a large body of opinion which supported the claim. The solicitors acting for the Medical Protection Society, which provided insurance for medical liability, handled the case. They obtained many opinions. After a few years, I visited their office and one of the questions I asked was how much their services had cost to that date. The solicitor looked at the file on the shelf and measured its thickness with finger and thumb. 'Oh, about $30,000,' he said with an expressionless voice. My reaction was one of cynicism, an attitude which unhappily continued with my experiences of the legal profession.

After what seemed like an eternity, I was told that they had heard from a most eminent paediatrician in Sheffield, England. This gentleman's opinion was that it was definitely not possible at four weeks of age to predict the onset of cerebral palsy. The plaintiffs accepted this advice, a smallish sum was agreed upon in compensation and the case was closed, but not without large legal expenses.

I must at this point include what I can call a straightforward claim. I admitted error in performing a sterilisation operation. It was the application of clips onto the Fallopian tubes via the laparoscope. The operation was done a couple of months after a baby was born. The normal procedure is to take a photograph of each tube with the clip in place at the conclusion of the operation. The view I had demonstrated that the tubes were occluded. But had I inspected them from a different angle I should have seen that one tube was not occluded. The patient conceived again and tragically the baby was born with a serious congenital abnormally. The claim was for a wrongful birth and was settled out of court.

It must be noted that a failure rate of 1: 300 was accepted for that sterilisation procedure and patients are warned about this beforehand. Nevertheless that fact is not acceptable in defence of a claim.

And now for the big one. Hold onto your seat...I was delivered a claim for $15 million. This was for a severely handicapped child who had congenital hydrocephalus, water on the brain. It was alleged that I should have diagnosed the abnormality three to four weeks before the due date, delivered the child early and that the outcome would have been better.

I was asked to see the mother four weeks before she was expecting her second baby to exclude an unstable lie. This is a not uncommon situation when, in the last month of pregnancy, the baby's position, or lie, within the womb changes. On the first visit, the baby's head was pointing downwards but was deflected towards the right side and therefore was not in a stable position. I asked her to return in five days for review. At this stage, the baby's head was central and pointing downwards. That means it was in a normal position. It remained in the normal position at every subsequent examination, thus excluding an unstable lie. Although the mother had had three normal ultrasound scans earlier in the pregnancy, the last being at 24 weeks, it was alleged that I should have ordered a fourth scan and thereby made the diagnosis of congenital hydrocephalus. That enlarged the head and made it more likely not to adopt a stable position in the womb. The case rested on whether or not there was an indication to order a scan. I and my expect witnesses argued there was no such indication. The plaintiff's lawyers argued the opposite.

The other issue in this case was whether an early delivery would have made any significant difference to the disability. It had been suggested that delivery three weeks early would have afforded a more successful outcome to the shunt procedure for the hydrocephalus.

Several years went by during which numerous expert opinions and counter-opinions were sought. The medical insurance company, on the advice of their lawyers, felt the case should be vigorously defended. They felt that there was a good chance a judge would find in their favour and therefore the case came to court.

Ten years had now elapsed since the baby was born. The defence therefore had to rely on the contemporaneous notes and what was accepted practice at the time. I certainly had no recollection of the individual consultations with the mother. Some of the lawyers expected me to remember what I said to the mother. I explained that had there been an unusual complication or a particular drama I would remember the occasion in detail, as indeed I often did. But I would conclude that the visits of this particular patient were not at all out of the ordinary.

As there was a large claim the case was heard in the Supreme Court in Phillip Street in Sydney. I did not hear all the evidence being given and went to the court on three days only. The first was to hear the testimony of the mother. That was important because counsel would refer to what she said when I was being cross-examined. She gave a detailed description of the first consultation with me. I wondered how she could possibly remember what I said after a lapse of ten years. She described me as a patronising doctor peering over his glasses. That last detail I knew was wrong as I had bifocal lenses and my distant vision was the main problem at that time. Therefore to be able to see her properly I would need to have the spectacles firmly pushed against the bridge of my nose. I pointed out this seeming error in her description to the judge and counsel when it was my turn to speak, but neither seemed interested. I thought there were further discrepancies in the mother's testimony, particularly when she alleged that I raised the issue of another scan at the first consultation. That would not have been on my mind.

The priority was to check the baby's position in the womb and that was arranged for five days later.

The overall tenure of the mother's testimony suggested that she had words put into her mouth by her lawyer. At least, that is how it appeared to me. But I could understand that they wanted to make as strong a case as possible. The family doubtless were desperate for more financial assistance and must have realised that the chances of winning the case were not good.

A whole day was allocated to my appearance at the witness stand. Actually the judge advised I sit. The plaintiff's barrister tried all sorts of tricks. His job was to discredit me. But in doing so he made some more errors of fact. First he introduced me as junior to the patient's GP. He stated that the GP had welcomed me into my specialist practice whereas it was the other way round. He is about ten years younger and arrived in the district as a very junior GP some years after I started my specialist practice there.

The barrister showed me the patient's own antenatal record card. I had made entries using a fountain pen and at the bottom of the card there were parts of several lines which had been washed off and then re-written. I immediately smelt a rat! Actually there would have been an unpleasant odour when the card was retrieved from the lady's handbag ten years previously! I felt sure the barrister was hoping to accuse me of falsifying the record. He stood there with his arms outstretched and with his black gown draped over them. With a voracious look on his face, he looked like a vulture about to swoop on some hapless, moribund prey. His two assistants, like curious magpies, were also looking expectantly for their senior's reward. The judge was craning his neck to get a better look at the card. So I deliberately addressed him and pointed out a yellow stain forming an arc at the edge of the affected area. I said, so as not to offend his sensibilities, that there had been an accident and part of the record had been washed off with some fluid. The judge immediately added that it was probably coffee; but I knew it was more likely to be urine. The specimen jars supplied by the pathologists were notorious for leaking and if the record card were placed next to the jar in the handbag an accident of this kind was likely to happen. At that point, the barrister changed the subject. He would swoop again.

Then the barrister turned his attention to the hospital record of the mother's attendance five days after the first consultation. I saw her in the maternity ward. As it was a public holiday my rooms were closed. I had warned her that if we confirmed an unstable lie she would be admitted for observation. The first entry on the record for that day was "Seen? Unstable lie" in what I thought was very reasonable handwriting. It did not, in my opinion, require the services of a pharmacist to read it! The "vulture" begged to differ. He was adamant that instead of "seen" it could read "scan". I stated as strongly as I could that that would not make sense. He tried to get me to admit that I intended to order a scan, but never actually carried out that order. The truth is that a non-urgent scan would not have been available on a public holiday, and I would not have brought the patient into the maternity ward for that purpose. Scans were performed in the medical imaging department. As it was I excluded an unstable lie and a scan was not indicated.

The third time I attended the court was when the obstetric expert witnesses were questioned. There were three appearing for me, all very well-respected senior men in active practice in Sydney. On the plaintiffs side was one retired Australian obstetrician and a retired English obstetrician who was making a new career as a free-lance expert witness. I have no doubt it was very costly bringing him out from London. His popularity with the lawyers was because he had the gift of convincing the judge by his eloquence and smooth talking. While he was postulating that there was more to this case than was recorded in the patient's records, I was furiously sending billet-doux forward to my counsel pointing out how ridiculous his ideas were. It was to no avail. The judge fell for his smooth talk.

There was a delay of about four months before the judgement was handed down. The judge concluded that a delivery three weeks early would not have made any significant difference to the outcome. This was based on expert advice from paediatricians, neurologists and neurosurgeons. On this basis, the award was a mere pittance compared to the $15 million claim.

The judge found against me. He took the view of the smooth-talking Englishman that there must have been more to the case than was recorded in the notes and therefore I should most definitely have ordered an ultrasound scan and confirmed a prenatal diagnosis. This disturbed me. I looked at the issue philosophically and felt the judge was looking for a way to help the family in their distress. During the hearing, the parents and the handicapped child were present towards the back of the court room. From his elevated position, the judge would clearly see the child writhing on the floor from time to time. He could not help but be touched by this distressing sight. He would have felt an enormous pressure to help the family if he could. Certainly, he would want to spare them a huge financial disadvantage.

The judge was, I presumed, torn between justice and mercy. The long delay in reaching a judgement must have meant it was for him a very difficult decision. By finding against me, he was able to save the family from the legal costs which would have amounted to $300,000 to $400,000!

My three expert witnesses were naturally alarmed at the judgement and one of them felt strongly that I should appeal. I conferred with my lawyer and was advised against it. I was told it would be long and arduous and very likely would not succeed. My cynicism rose to fever pitch when the concluding remark from the lawyer was, 'It's only a game.' How disgraceful! No wonder the relationship between doctors and lawyers is often strained. And I supposed that part of "the game" was the insulting way I was treated by the plaintiff's barrister. I mentioned this to my lawyer too. And she said he is paid to do that and "when that case is finished he will be busy insulting the next defendant".

Any case that comes to court can have the potential of wider ramifications. The judgement often sets a precedent. That thought obviously was in the mind of my friendly expert witness who urged me to appeal. He was concerned that it would be difficult to defend future cases of a similar nature.

I made an attempt at lobbying for change in the investigation and management of medical malpractice. The "no fault" system in New Zealand seems to me much more helpful than the system which currently operates in Australia. Disability is handled in NZ by a compensation mechanism which does not involve the courts. Possible malpractice is handled by robust medical peer review and where fault is established a tribunal determines appropriate disciplinary action. As it is, in this country, proper management of malpractice is delayed or even prevented by a pending compensation case.

Financial support can now be obtained through the National Disability Insurance Scheme (NDIS). But I understand it was at first swamped by a proliferation of autism cases and it ran out of money to help those with the sort of disability which I have recorded. Hopefully that problem has now been resolved and the NDIS can supply the needs of those who would otherwise sue their medical attendant. Unfortunately there remains strong opposition to a "no fault" system from the legal profession in Australia.

The experience of a defendant in court is not one which fades from memory in a hurry. In my case, much prolonged thinking ensued. There were plenty of "what ifs". What if I was more eloquent in my answers to questions, particularly to the cross-examination by the plaintiff's barrister? What if I remembered more detail of my consultations with the patient?

Chewing over the "what ifs" only leads to more anxiety. So when I came to terms with the judgement I needed to find consolation elsewhere.

So how was I to find consolation in the face of a seemingly unfair judgement? A comforting quotation came to mind. 'Come to me all you that are weary and are carrying heavy burdens and I will give you rest.'[29]According to the scholar, Prof R.V.G. Tasker, "rest" carries the sense of

---

[29] Matthew 11:28 New Revised standard Version.

"relief", relief from crippling anxiety and relief (most importantly) from a sin-laden conscience.

The speaker is Jesus. he is contrasting the burdensome obligations imposed by the Pharisees and teachers of the law with the refreshing new way which He offers in relationship with Him. The rest or relief He offers is made possible by His sacrifice on the cross of Calvary. His forgiveness grants reconciliation with God. He has at the same time condemned the sin and restored the sinner.

Let's consider the judge's position. Is it possible for him to satisfy both parties, the plaintiff and the defendant? That is plainly a ridiculous question. The judge must find in favour of one or the other, not both. The only way he could satisfy both would be to pay the compensation out of his own pocket. That would render him bankrupt very smartly!

We deserve to be punished for our rebellion against God. But God forgives the penitent because Jesus paid the penalty for our sin when he sacrificed Himself at Calvary. So God delivered both justice and mercy at the same time. Jesus did and continues to do what no human judge can do. That is a most joyful consolation. For that, I am eternally grateful.

Conclusion

I have enjoyed a privileged life. That conviction has rested on three distinct assurances. The first is that my life has been built on loving and lasting relationships with my family and close friends. The second is that the rock on which those relationships are founded is the love of God. And the last is the conviction that Jesus has given me His Spirit to teach, empower and sustain me.

It is said that at the heart of every human being is a god-shaped hole. By that, it is meant that we are all created and designed for fellowship with God. That conviction has been present since ancient times. It has been expressed in various ways over the ages. For example, when the Apostle Paul said to the Athenians, 'In Him we live and move and have our being'[30] he ascribed that saying to the Cretan philosopher-poet, Epimenides. In front of the Areopagus, the Apostle alerted his audience to an inscription on an altar which read "To an unknown god"[31]. He proclaimed this god to be the creator of all things and the one who has appointed Jesus to judge the whole world. He also quoted the Cilician

---

[30] Acts 17: 28 New revised standard version of the Bible.

[31] Acts 17: 23 New revised standard version of the Bible.

stoic philosopher, Aratus, who wrote "We too are his offspring"[32]. The Apostle thus pointed to that unrealised and subconscious truth. Humans have a potential relationship with God which is realised through repentance and belief in the Gospel. There is always an urgency to turn back to God and Paul called on his hearers to repent there and then[33]. He expressed the same urgency to the Corinthians when he wrote "Now is the acceptable time; now is the day of salvation!"[34] None of us knows when for us it may be too late. We must make peace with God as soon as possible. None of us knows when we might die.

What we believe is very important; but who and whose we are is even more important. I am so grateful that my seminal experience as a student became the bedrock truth to hold onto for the rest of my life. What was revealed to me on that day in 1961 was a genuine epiphany. As I explained in, "A Beginning", Jesus revealed Himself in His word as recorded by St Luke. Using the words of the prophet Isaiah[6] His proclamation in the synagogue at Nazareth convinced me of the freedom he declared. Also it was a confirmation of the loving and lasting relationship which God in Christ had given me. My god-shaped hole was filled with the reality of knowing Jesus.

The second collect in Morning Prayer[35] reads, 'O God...whose service is perfect freedom...' This is both one of the great characteristics and one of the paradoxes of the

---

[32] Acts 17: 29 New revised standard version of the Bible.

[33] Acts 17: 30 New revised standard version of the Bible.

[34] 2 Corinthians 6:2 New revised standard version of the Bible.

[35] An Australian Prayer Book 1978 p. 28

Christian faith. The clever man with atheistic leanings will ask how can you have a set of strict laws, be completely obedient and still be free. To answer his question you have to direct him to the alternatives.

Ask him about the anarchist who wants to run the country without any organised government. A quick glance at history will demonstrate the result of anarchist movements. Is that real freedom?

Ask him about young people who leave conventional society and join a commune where the doctrine includes "free love". When the dream turns sour, is that real freedom?

Ask him about the child brought up without real discipline and free to do just as he pleases. He finds himself caught up in an endless round of pleasure-seeking activities with no lasting aims. Is that real freedom?

Then ask him to look back at the Christian and enquire about his life. The Christian will say he is free because he follows not so much a set of rules, but a person. The Christian is freed from the details of the written code because the Holy Spirit guides and instructs him. Freedom for the Christian involves a living relationship with his Lord, Jesus Christ. He has an irresistible desire to be filled with the Spirit Jesus has promised. The Apostle Paul repeatedly referred to this as being "In Christ".

Freedom is manifold. First the new Christian is amazed that he is set free from guilt and shame. The written code confirms his guilt. Faith in Christ removes that guilt. The Apostle Paul wrote, 'For the wages of sin is death, but the free gift of God is eternal life in Christ Jesus our Lord.'[36] It

---

[36] Romans 6: 23 New revised standard version of the Bible.

is indeed the "amazing grace" of our lord Jesus Christ that Confers that free gift. That amazing grace was explained to me on the steps of Guy's hospital by my friend Peter. And I received that free gift and began a journey as a disciple of Christ.

The concept of freedom was revealed to me not many days later. The "good news" which Jesus enunciated, as he read from the prophet Isaiah[37] meant much more than freedom from guilt and shame. It next meant the freedom to love as Christ has loved us. His grace has freed us from those things that block that love.

A former neighbour was a child of the colonial era. He was brought up under the British Raj. He told me one day that one did not speak to those above one's station and one did not speak to those below one's station. One only befriended those who were at the same social level as oneself. How sad!

Racial prejudice was also ingrained in previous generations. I remember walking down the street with a great aunt many years ago. She pointed to a couple across the street and in an obviously sneering way said, 'See those people. They are a bit jewy!' By that she meant they were despised, and she obviously despised their race. That same generation also looked on the African races as inferior. Prejudice and selfishness are both alive and well, inhibiting all love for those with whom we do not belong. But our multicultural society has helped, to some degree, to reduce racial tension.

---

[37] Luke 4: 18 New revised standard version of the Bible.

From a young age, my experiences taught me to relate to all strata of society as equals. That is so important in the healing profession. Jesus gave equal attention to everyone in need regardless of their status. He taught us that His heavenly Father loves each and every one without distinction.

In my village primary school class, I mixed with village yokels. I also shared accommodation in a little old cottage with a young cockney lad from East London. A prim and proper aunt was aghast when she heard me speaking with a broad country accent! As a medical student I was introduced to high society. A paediatric specialist, a senior consultant, took us, his tutorial group, to dinner one evening to the Athenaeum. That is arguably the most prestigious gentleman's club in London town. Members past and present include prime ministers and archbishops. On another occasion, I was travelling on the overnight train from Inverness to King's cross, London. I was joined in the dining car by a lady who claimed to be a countess and certainly spoke and acted the part. I must add that after the meal she retreated to her first-class sleeper, whilst I slunk off to my third-class sitter!

Helping the police with their enquiries taught me to listen and understand, to respect and to love. No matter what a person has done there is no one who is excluded from God's redeeming love.

The freedom Christ gives frees us from social and religious prejudice. It frees us from petty jealousy, from bickering and misunderstandings. Describing the love Jesus expressed the Apostle Paul wrote, 'Love is patient; love is kind; love is not envious or boastful or arrogant or rude. It does not insist on its own way; it is not irritable or resentful; it does not rejoice in wrongdoing but rejoices in the truth.'[38]

Before I was a Christian, I would never have the confidence to show compassion to someone who was not already a close friend. I was in any case naturally shy. But the freedom that Christ had brought me broke down the barriers of prejudice and reserve. As a doctor, Christ enabled me to show compassion to the unlovely. Even to those who would wish me harm, such as the lady who threatened my life with a knife and a firearm, I felt no antipathy. Only the grace of Christ could grant such freedom. This freedom compels us, urges us, to get alongside those who cry out for Christ's love. As a physician I was compelled to agree that every one of my patients was equally in need and equally deserving of that love. But I am sure I failed repeatedly to fully meet their deepest need. Only Jesus could do that.

I was always aware that there is no barrier to extend the sort of love which Jesus had extended to me. That even included the young man who killed my friend and nearly killed me in the road accident. Rendering love to that man meant expressing genuine forgiveness. I am constantly reminded of Archbishop Desmond Tutu's wise words, 'There is no future without forgiveness.' In both the daily little incursions as well as the major attacks on our security, forgiveness is so important, actually vital, to preserve good relationships.

On a personal level, I felt free to love the young lady I would marry. Parents in every society give advice to their children about marriage. In some societies, the young couple

---

[38] 1 Corinthians 13: 4–6 New revised standard version of the Bible.

have no choice. My own father (who was 10,000 miles away in Australia at the time) was very keen to intervene and wanted me to wait till he had made his own enquiries. While I appreciated his advice, I felt strongly that the major party in rendering guidance was the Holy Spirit.

I had been blessed with five younger sisters and had experienced and appreciated female company at medical school; but did not develop any romantic relationships at that time. When I left there, I cannot remember the search for a life-long partner being a particular priority. But I was "surprised by joy". My first hospital appointment was as a house surgeon at St Richard's[39] in Chichester, Sussex. I could have gone to another hospital. In fact, I very nearly went to Exeter in Devon. I believe there was divine intervention. On one of the wards at St Richard's, I met a nurse, Daphne, to whom I was immediately attracted. It was love at first sight. Surely it was divinely ordained. I should quote Shakespeare at this point because, 'Oh, she doth teach the torches to burn bright.'[40] She stood out immediately as a gift from heaven. She is my life's partner, and we are enjoying our fifty-seventh year of happy marriage. Yes, I am confident that it was the Lord's doing that I was led to meet her and that therein was freedom.

I believe the single gynaecologist is at a massive disadvantage. The experience learnt in a godly marriage helps enormously to relate appropriately to female patients, especially when they present with a variety of deep emotional problems.

---

[39] Richard was a bishop of Chichester in the thirteenth century.
[40] Romeo and Juliet – Act 1 scene 5

Our marriage has been blessed with the arrival of three children and all three enjoy the exciting and fulfilling paths the Lord has given them to follow. We now have the joy of watching six beautiful grandchildren taking their God-given paths onto the world stage.

Another aspect of the freedom Jesus has given is the freedom to serve. In secular society, there are prescribed career paths. Unfortunately, those paths are sometimes strewn with serious obstacles. For example, a close relative and a friend have both complained about workplace bullying. They were in completely unrelated situations. In both cases, the outcomes were the dismissal of the complainants, leaving the culprits free to continue their unwelcome habits. Both these complainants are Christians. Both feel free to serve in a different capacity without pursuing recrimination. In my litigation case, it was important that I should draw on the well of God's grace to accept the judgment against me, however hard it seemed at the time. In all those circumstances, it is the indwelling Spirit who gives confidence and courage to rise above injustice and resume service wherever the Spirit leads. That is freedom.

In both the litigation case and in my annus horribilis, consolation was found in Christ's rest. Although in the latter case that seemed far off at the time the promised, rest did eventually come as relief from anxiety and provided hope for the future.

The Holy Spirit may guide you to serve in a different capacity or in a totally different location. That may be contrary to financial or social considerations. But if there is an inner conviction of the rightness of the change in direction a sense of freedom will supervene.

There is supremely a sense of freedom for the Christian who engages in voluntary service. That applies especially after retirement from one's paid occupation. The Christian is invited to be fruitful in old age as Psalm 92 states[41]. There is a glorious sense of freedom when engaging in various ministries after retirement. It is a privilege, for example, to offer pastoral care to those less fortunate than oneself both in hospitals and in prison. It is a ministry full of great moments of encouragements. On one occasion, I was called to the bedside of a dear lady who was not on my list. The system we worked with was to only see those who were of one's own denomination and asked for a visit. As I passed this lady's door she called out and invited me in. Then she said, 'I have been praying that you would come. And now you are here!' She was a Catholic and I am an Anglican. She evidently had been a patient of mine and must have felt blessed by that professional relationship. On this occasion, she desperately wanted me to pray with her. That was a great privilege, and it gave her great comfort.

The word "joy" appears frequently in the New Testament. The prime example is the word of Jesus when he promised his disciples they would be filled with joy when he rose from the dead.[42] The Christian always has cause to rejoice. It is another aspect of freedom. In this instance he is free to enter into that glorious Presence which that implies. Even in crises there is room for praise because he is blessed

[41] Psalm 92: 12–15 New revised standard version of the Bible.

[42] John 16:20 New revised standard version of the Bible.

with hope. While I was recovering from my accident, there was much to be thankful for. I was blessed by the constant ministry of my wife and family and by the kindness of so many Christian friends. There was time to take stock and review my life's journey. There was the freedom to express myself and the Lord blessed me with an increase in faith as He delivered me through that crisis. Similarly, although my *annus horribilis* severely diminished my faith, hope was not totally abandoned and there was much rejoicing as the year ended.

As we age the time for eternal rejoicing draws closer. Nothing will impede its coming and nothing will impair its fulfilment.

I was blessed a couple of years ago by meeting a gentleman in hospital aged 93. His medical condition was not on the top of his agenda. Instead he was keen to tell me about his past and his current joy. He had been a journalist posted to Cooma in the '50s and '60s. He reported regularly on the progress of the Snowy Mountain scheme. He was a man of faith and he had duties as a lay reader in the Anglican Church. And then he said something remarkable. He had a radiant smile and the demeanour of confident rest. He clearly rejoiced in his close relationship with his Lord and Saviour because he said, 'I think I am in heaven now.' That man would not have realised that he ministered to me as well. He caused me in that moment to be very thankful to Jesus.

The most profound and valuable gift that anyone can receive is the gift of the Holy Spirit. That is why Luke records Jesus saying, 'If you then, who are evil, know how to give good gifts to your children, how much more will the heavenly Father give the Holy Spirit to those who ask Him.'[43]

And that is why at Pentecost Peter exclaims, 'Repent and be baptised every one of you in the name of Jesus Christ so that your sins may be forgiven; **and you will receive the gift of the Holy Spirit**.'[44] Surely this is the quintessential aspect of life as a Christian, life in Christ.

The Holy Spirit has been my constant guide, comforter, friend and tutor. I am not saying I have been a perfect student, far from it. But I say that He has always been there. He has never given up on me. He it is who has taught me how to relate to those who are not easy to talk to. He it is who has given me strength in difficult circumstances. He it is who has always reminded me that forgiveness is always available for my failings. It is he who has reminded me that I must forgive, without hesitation, those who have hurt me. He it is who has reminded me that I owe Jesus my contrition, my thanks, my weak love, my all

---

[43] Luke 11: 13 New revised standard version of the Bible.
[44] Acts 2: 38 New revised standard version of the Bible.

St Richard of Chichester is best known for his prayer.

Thanks be to thee Lord Jesus Christ,
for all the benefits which thou hast won for us,
for all the pains and insults which thou hast borne for us.
O most merciful Redeemer, Friend and Brother,
may we know thee more clearly,
love thee more dearly
and follow thee more nearly, day by day.

Printed in Australia
Ingram Content Group Australia Pty Ltd
AUHW011826120224
390311AU00003B/24

9 781035 800216